SEASONS OF THE SOUL

SHELBY KOTTEMANN

SEASONS OF THE SOUL

Copyright © 2022 by Shelby Kottemann

Willow Tree Press
Wisconsin, US 53572

All rights reserved. No part of this publication may be reproduced distributed or transmitted in any form or by any means including photocopying recording or other electronic or mechanical means without proper written permission of author or publisher, except in the case of brief quotations embodied in critical reviews and certain other noncommercial uses permitted by copyright law.

ISBN 978-1-7379087-2-2 (paperback)
ISBN 978-1-7379087-3-9 (hardcover)

Printed in the United States of America.

What People Are Saying

"This book will quiet your soul. It is a comfort that draws you into heart space and reverence."

—**Jean Walters, International Best Selling Author**

"With descriptive, powerful art in her words and pictures, she gives structure and empowerment to mind, body and soul."

—**Toni Stone Bruce, CEO/Founder of Precious Stones 4 Life, LLC**

"As the Author Shelby Kottemann writes about life, she poetically does so with the essence of nature and the four seasons."

—**Karen Wright, International Best Selling Author, Radio Host**

"Thought provoking and whimsical, the author shares a vibrant tapestry of nature and what it teaches us about ourselves as we grow."

—**Aeriol Ascher, MsD, Positive Vibes with Aeriol Host & Body MindSoul.TV founder**

"Once again, Shelby has masterfully used nature and faith to teach deep life lessons."

—**Elda Robinson, International Bestselling Author**

Table of Contents

Prologue *7*

Part I. *Fall* *9*

Part II. *Winter* *49*

Part III. *Spring* *89*

Part IV. *Summer* *125*

Epilogue *171*

Prologue

Have you ever noticed? Life happens in seasons.

There is a structure to life that I can lean into. It provides a purposeful, simple, profound framework to the continual trials I face. As with most things I believe, this structure is connected to nature. I call it the seasons of the soul.

There's autumn when, just as leaves fall and trees are left bare, we are faced with sudden change, hollowing loss, or harvest. In any aspect of life, we can experience autumn, and it doesn't always happen in September.

Autumn turns to winter, when we move beyond transitions and begin to integrate change into the landscape of our hearts. Like in nature, winter requires the hibernation of going within, the strength of diligence, and the willingness to hold faith.

Spring is when we begin to apply all we've discovered in ourselves to the way we move in the world. Like a flower sprouting from warming soil, spring is the time to grow into who we've become.

That brings us to summer. In summer, we glow in the warmth of deepened love. Through all the ways we've grown, there is a sense of fulfillment that comes in the gratitude we hold for ourselves, life's process, and God. We take it in.

By looking at life like the continuous rhythm of nature's seasons, I find reassurance that hard times won't be forever. I anticipate the strength required of me. I realize new growth comes from faith and determination. And I cherish the times when life is at ease, knowing all seasons are temporary.

The seasons of nature don't always match the ones happening in our lives. We can be diving through a winter in the midst of warm sunny days. Or feeling the inner glow of summer when snow is falling.

By looking at life in this way, I find that I can lean on nature when I'm seeking a depth of support not found in man. God designs nature to hold us in this way. Journey through the seasons with me. Begin at whichever season you're in. Lean into your faith in the seasons of your soul.

PART I.
FALL

Introduction

Autumn is a time we might feel a sense of shock. As the cold wind meets mature leaves, suddenly something is ending.

Endings can feel like a death. When trees lose their leaves, they appear barren. As we encounter loss or change, we can meet the same feelings. But know that just as fall is preparing the trees, God is preparing you. You're on the cusp of a soul's journey on which you will grow to new heights. The best we can do in this phase is surrender our leaves to the wind.

Trust is a big part of autumn's process. Trust in what is falling away; that it will grow something new. Trust that you have what it takes to meet change with a sense of purpose. Trust that God will guide you so long as you seek Him.

When we embrace change, faith embraces us.

Evolve

I used to love looking out onto the field beside my home. The tendrils and boughs of grass soothe my spirit as I soak in the view. And in the winter, when their brown stalks and fuzzy blossoms are nested in a fresh blanket of snow, there's a sense of romantic peace in watching them slowly sway in the cold north breeze.

Then one day, a man came in on large equipment with a force much like that breeze. In that day, he eradicated the field of wildflowers and tall grasses I'd come to love so. Gone was a peaceful place.

The man nor the owner who directed him couldn't know how special their place was just naturally. As it's told, beauty, and also worth, is in the eye of the beholder.

Over a year went by. I looked out on that field, first with disappointment, but then in interest. I was watching a transformation take place. Nature was taking it back. Another well-known truth of our world. Yet it spoke another truth to me because I was walking the same path as that field. Rebuilding.

There are times in our lives when a man or a woman or a thing comes in. Invades and destructs the pure beauty and peace that once was. Reasons vary. To dwell on why is a drain and a waste. Sometimes, like the field, worth is not aptly seen. In other cases, it's sheer chance.

But I don't believe in coincidence. I believe in synchronicity. I believe in opportunity. And with every challenge comes the choice to find one. When we face times of destruction in our lives, we are met equally with challenge. Ready or not, someone above believes we are.

When we choose to dwell, we stay in that challenge, that destruction, for a lifetime. When we make the choice to take the path to rebuild or in any case, like the field, regrow, we lift ourselves from the soil anew. The same yet different.

Re-growing is not starting over, mind you. For if you remember the field, you know it regrew once its bearings had changed. That makes it stronger, wiser, the same yet reformed. Like us, the field adapts.

When we choose to regrow, we rise up from changed soil with new nutrients for success. New sensitivities, strengths, awarenesses that before were yet unknown. When we rise again, we are as beautiful and peaceful as we've ever been. Only this time, we're refined, a new edition, better fit for our world.

In this sense, could it be said that destruction is a gift? Maybe not. But it is necessary for us to transform the greatest parts of ourselves. Because without it, how would our hearts evolve?

Faithful Flying

There's something magical about the way an eagle flies. My first Native American friend told me you can always tell an eagle by the way it flies. The shape of their wings in the sky is different from any other bird. Back then, I could only aspire to be so attuned. So I practiced.

Today, I can spot a bald eagle from fields away. Rewarded for my practice, I understand exactly what he meant. An eagle doesn't just beat its feathers. It soars and glides through the sky. It's as if those wings are sails for the powerful ship that is its body, steering its course through the crystal blue light of the day, riding the shifting tides of the wind.

Perception holds the keys to our seeing what lies before us. When we see deeply, an eagle teaches us a lot through the way it flies. By passing glance, some could see a bird casually coasting through the day, looking down on its kingdom below. Others might see a wild one rising through the trees and up. It chooses not to press against the changing winds but rather rides them masterfully over the forest to take in the world from its view.

The winds of change are a dependable part of life and nature. The eagle is unlike many birds seen tumbling and rushing, pushing and flailing, going nowhere in the wind as they fight to carry on the route of their plan. No, the eagle, this force of nature, harnesses the push of the gusts. Without resistance, it meets the unstoppable might of the wind with the honed practice of its lift and coast, taking it to where it was best to land all along. In this elegant craft, eagles show us just how to glide through winds of change, no matter how gentle or roaring, with an awe-inducing grace.

Within each of us lies the potential to find this eagle. Imagine. Feel the wind blow all around your skin, your hair, in essence your feathers and your wings. It's riveting. It overcomes you with its energy, the power that is unstoppable and ever moving, body and spirit. It calls you to follow its flow, feel its shifts of change.

When you give rise to flight, you become a symbol of strength, courage, power, and freedom. It seems like that soar shows exactly how.

How it takes strength of character to rise above. But when you do, you certainly get a broader view of the forest, when before you were lost in the trees. From those crystal blue skies above, you see even yourself more clearly.

How courage is required all for the leap off the branch, for once you're sailing the uplifting, shifting tides of the wind, something larger is at hand to show you the way. It soothes you, awakens you, empowers you.

Wind may die low or surge through the sky, making you feel all alone in that vast crystal blue horizon. But you are not alone. You are never alone. For the same force that churns the air is guiding your course. Giving you everything you need to build deep from within.

The expression of all that you build is in your mastery of soaring; in your harnessing of the wind. Harnessing the power to set your own course, the right course, the one that follows the sense deep inside you. The sense that stirs you to speak, to move, to act, to still. Your power is seated in every great and tiny following of that sense. You feel it when you move.

As you move your way, I love your freedom most of all. Like the power of a vigilant soldier in the wake of sacrifice, or the valiance of a step through an unknown door, freedom is bred from faith. It's a faith in knowing that your wings are not the only things that fuel your course, that something omnipotent supports your greater way. Just like the wind, it blows below you, behind you, above and around, encompassing you in the love and force you need the most. Accept it, have faith in it, soar in it, for the freedom of flying comes from faith.

Through that faith, the eagle's freedom is found in a more all-encompassing way. It's found by the magnificent blend of power that can only be born from Grace. Grace gives you the small voice to hear, to feel, to know, to steer your course. It tells you the route to follow as you ride the wind. It sets your course with rest when you have no wind at all to push you. Power grows stronger each time you have the strength and the courage to follow your knowing. It grows more firmly seated alongside the growth of your faith in yourself, of your faith in God. And once you harness those skills, you discover that they were all connected, just as they have been within this bird.

So what allows the eagle to soar so gracefully, unlike any other of its kind, is it's willing to give up its will. It shows a trust in the forces that guide it. It teaches us to remember that He'll carry you where you're meant to be how you were meant to go so long as you harness the wind.

A few strong wing beats and it's on its way again. Like a team, the wind and the wings. When we harness life this way, faith, no matter the weather, I believe we uncover the many dimensions of our inner eagle. We come to know that when we see that striking silhouette in the sky, there's something far deeper about their difference.

Autumn's Release

As I stepped out into the morning dew, I saw with clearer eyes. I felt a renewed tenderness that greeted me like a long-missed part of myself. The growing number of leaves sprinkled across the ground had grown even since yesterday, not just in number but diversity. Their shapes and colors marking each tree's letting go of its own year of fighting for life and strength and light for a long and dormant rest, a faithful wait for renewal, new growth reaching farther and taller than yet before.

Cascading down in a multitude of colors. Some of those falling catch your eye for they are special, colors only God can make. The colors and shapes of them show just how many ways there are to let go.

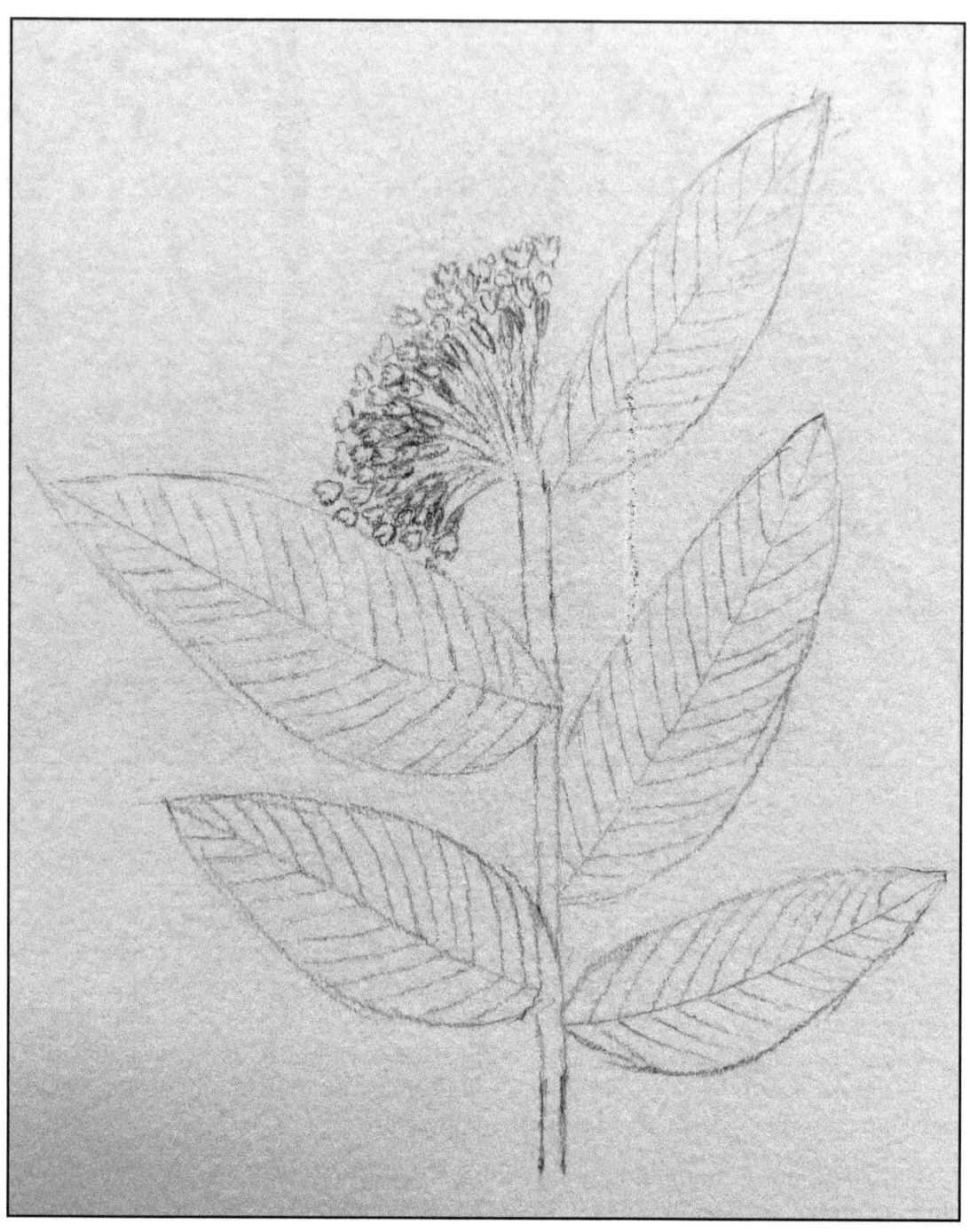

God's Work in Milkweeds

A weed can be a flower of sorts. A lot of things I believe are defined more by a person's perspective than what they really are. Milkweed, for instance, is the only plant that feeds the monarch butterfly. In late spring, rosy purple flowers bloom from tall stems that fuel the regal ladies before they lay their eggs on their broad leaves. Then, when her babies emerge no larger than the length of your fingernail, the milk within those leaves fuels them to grow to just about the size of your whole finger. Making their gold-sealed cocoon on that very plant to emerge weeks later fanning wet wings to dry in the early morning sun. In the second World War, children collected pods to make flotation devices that saved soldiers' lives in combat. All this life-giving might in what we unwittingly regard as a weed.[1]

History in mind, I came upon these plants on my late autumn walk. As I saw them from a distance, they looked like a white wisp of Granny's hair atop a browning stalk so blackened it looked burnt. A far cry from the vibrant colors of spring, but yet it took center stage against the backdrop of the roadside.

In late autumn, when the case of a milkweed pod cracks open at the seam, it reveals a nest of silk-packed seeds inside. As I peered inside, there was something about them that took my breath away. Every single seed was arranged inside that pod in neat, tidy rows, like someone carefully packed them in there. Each silky puff was bound to the stalk at their tip so that as the pod unfolded, they opened up like synchronized swimmers in formation. Like little stars ready to blow away in the wind. God takes great care in putting even the smallest pod in order. And there's an art to the way it unfolds and lets go, ready to begin again. So many affirming truths in one mighty weed.

---

[1] https://www.endangered.org/milkweed-is-a-life-preserver-for-monarchs/

Decay

I walked alone in the woods, surrounded by the energy of thousands of trees. Yet it was one fallen oak that captivated me. Drying roots splayed out vertically from its place on the earth, symmetrically interwoven as if they'd never left the ground. They were black as night, a color that most often brings to mind death. The decay of this old oak wasn't a comfortable thing to look at. Sights like these unsettle and sadden. Just like the death and decay of eras in our lives or relationships in our hearts.

Decay is like the unpacking of emotions that come with goodbye. Decay is like the falling apart that we feel when we lose someone special. When this process happens inside us, the world doesn't always see. It's slow-moving and quiet, deep and transformative.

We must give grace to ourselves in times of decay. We must apply our strength to have faith while letting go. We must believe that a hole won't be in the earth or our hearts forever where something magical and alive once grew. Because slowly in this process, the birth of new love springs up, fresh and great from the roots that fueled it.

What was once wise and reverent never stops nourishing us, heart and soul. The remnants of this oak, falling softly back into the earth, are cultivating something new and beautiful. Bright yellow flowers spring forth, tall and tender in its wake. They were like a vision of life's polarities colliding in circular motion. Symbols of the way the beauties of our lives beget and build upon one another, especially in our hearts. Blossoms of the awakened faith that come from this process.

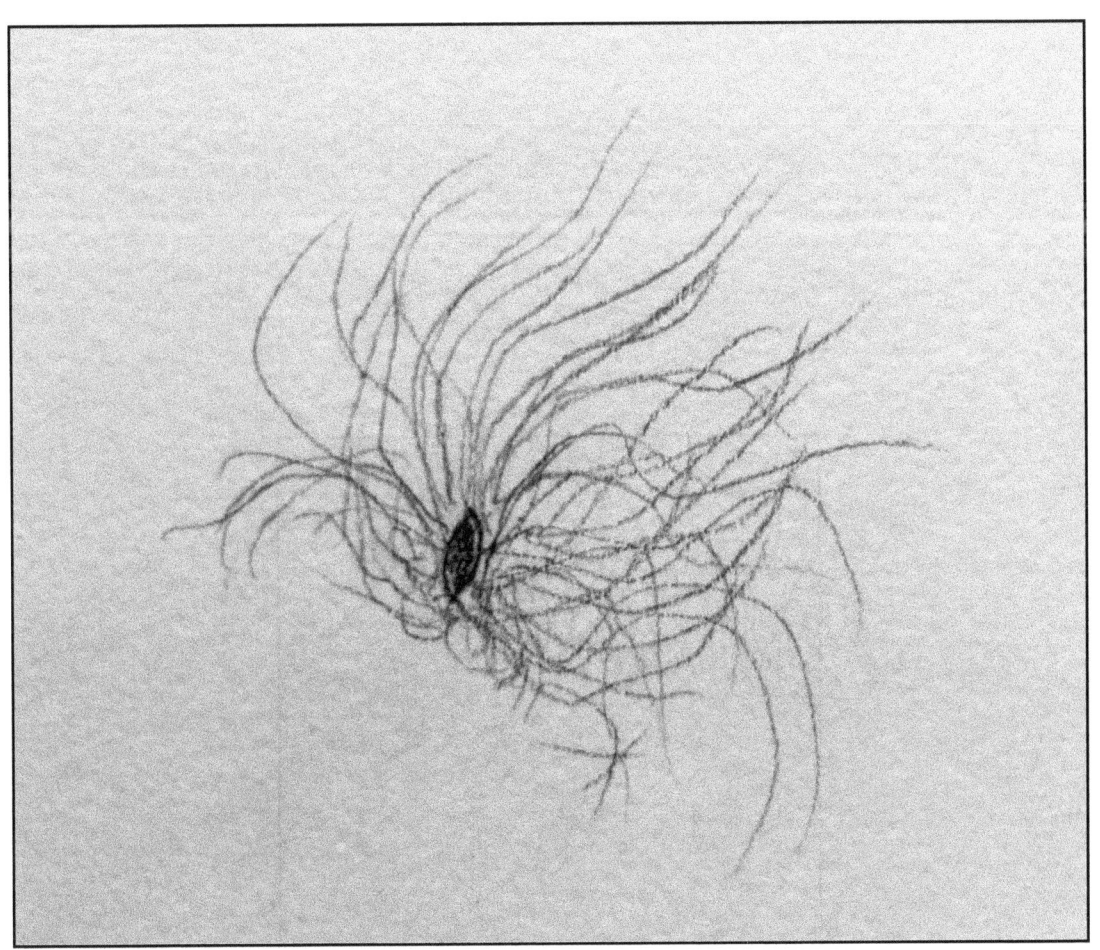

Cottonwood

A plough of white softness from the cottonwood tree floated through the air like a cloud of drifting snow lost in time. I reached out to touch one and caught it in my hand, pulling it close to see. In a moment, it flew from my fingers on a breeze, before I was ready to part from its softness. Sometimes, accepting beauty into our lives entails the promise of letting it go just the same, in its own time, with a cottonwood measure of grace.

Leaves

What if a tree held onto old growth? Like ours, it was once new and remarkable, especially to watch it unfold. But in hindsight, just on the dawn of letting go, when the tree prepares its goodbye to the season of life that had once been, that's when they look most beautiful of all.

It's as if autumn saves up all leaves' majesty to behold us with, making the sweetest end to a summer's reverie. So hard to say goodbye to such a beautiful thing, captivating for the fine nuances of every detail. I take them in as if each day's a goodbye, knowing their splendor is precious and fading in time. Never a glimmer taken at passing glance. In my heart forever, my mind's eye a lifetime, my spirit without end.

For if I stayed in their beauty forever, no room would be made. New growth would come, only to be met by the reverie of the past. A hallmark to true misery is the company of fellows whom you were once with. Together in a day. Sorrow reaches the bones of those who mourn tomorrow for what might have been.

But today holds promise. For the rising sun asks again that these leaves fulfill their call. Display to us the finer beauty of letting go. Bode us well as you cast down on your way. Grant us wishes for tomorrow when we see your buds come May.

Such a vulnerability it takes for that tree to stand bare from November through May. A lonely, barren, cold truth it stands through as a true sign of faith.

I remember as a child thinking winter trees look dead. Maybe in those barren times, parts of ourselves die with those magnificent leaves. But in all their glory cascading down, there's no greater truth than this: Whatever is let go, in whichever fashion, time, or day, is bound to bring new again. Water it, tend to it, your tree, and life will grow again.

Letting go seemed to have come in as many forms as there were colors of leaves on the iridescent trees. Grandma, friends, childhood home, the life I'd built all my life, places and people always known, moments gone by, so many little things.

Every time my grandma said, "Grandma loves you," in her kitchen by the carport door. Every crevice of their well-lived home of six decades or more. My friends and the adventures we lived in our own innocent ways. The folk that seemed like family found in the most unexpected places, as they so often are. My childhood home, the frame for our memories. The places no one knew meant something to me, but I did. For their solace in my day, their beauty. The spirit of every child whom I got to love. Routines and spontaneity that, come to think of it, comforted much. The bashful look and tenderness of one life-touching friend.

Sometimes, I live there in reverie. It leaves me knowing what that tree would feel if it didn't cast its colorful beauty in the fall. Dead things a branch holds onto poison it within, rob its nutrients, its joy, its wake and life and day until there's nothing left. Thank God He prunes our tree. For if not, we'd surely know by now the sorrow of yesterday's tomorrow.

It's hard. I live it now. But with each new day is another ray from the golden, rising sun. The same one that reaches into those leaves to cast them from each branch. What comes with it is nourishment in a form only dreams are made of.

Energy of the Heart

I spied the eagle, seated proudly atop the limb of its preferred tree. It looked over its kingdom of the lake, quietly spoken. Mesmerized, I watched as I coursed through the building waves. Those waves pressed me on, ne'er I get washed up the wrong shore, but oh how I didn't want to leave his graces. I found myself looking back, just to take a little moment more of him in. But the farther I pressed onward, the more forward my course steered, the greater I realized that on a paddle board the greater you look back, the more you lose your bearings and your balance. That was a truth about life I took with me as I reinvigorated my push to forge ahead. And when I looked back once more, his tree was gone from my view. Replaced was the bigger picture of the bay and all I'd found there.

The Barn

On our route to and from our favorite place, there are certain landmarks that punctuate how far we've come, how far we have to go. There's a bond that forms with these places just for the anticipation of seeing them as we travel our long, loved road.

It is the unique places that stay with me. Those places that are in essence, a form of expression, like the silo in the shape of a jack-o-lantern, or a cobalt blue barn in tribute to the dairy farmers 'round America.

But some places haunt me. They stick in my spirit. There is a barn on the highway that stands in disrepair. Holes in the roof. Boards broken in its walls. The structure was clearly falling apart. Someday, piece by piece, it will fall into the ground, a memory. History.

But when you consider the boards and shingles, the letters that adorn its front face, the cupolas resting atop, you envision it in all its glory. You fill in the pieces of its unknown past to sculpt together the story yet untold. It's a mystery of your making.

What will remain in my memory long after the image of its prime, beyond the time it falls down to the earth, what remains in my mind's eye, in my heart, are those holes in the roof where the light shines in. It makes me wonder at how there wouldn't be this flood of light in that old forgotten barn without its dilapidated hole. Just like the holes and cracks in our hearts are where the light pours in, without that "damage," there'd be no opportunity to fill that space with the bright effervescence of light. The Light that is Love in all its purest forms from Heaven.

What stays with me are those cracks in the walls, the gaping spaces that allow creatures in. Who knows what lives in that barn? But who knows what that barn gave a safe place to lie? To stay. Because walls aren't everything. And letting in isn't so bad. Sometimes, the creatures that made their way inside make a hollow place turn to home.

Those letters, some in place, some gone, some hanging on a nail. They tell a story of another time. I'll let your imagination fill in the details. Use the senses. Take your time. Explore the great unknown.

Lastly, there's the osprey who faithfully return to raise their young each year. To them, no time has passed. They've perched atop the cupola on that barn roof just as their parents who came before them. They've repaired their nest through the storms that put a hole in the roof. Tended their young as the boards cracked below. For this place is as traditional to them as it is to us. They knew this barn before it became old. They lived over it before we ever came. They depend on that barn and its cupola. And maybe, somehow, that barn, in all its times and stages, depends on those birds too. Perhaps it even looks out for us.

So you see, within the breaking of things lies the great opportunity for new light to pour in. From God above, from nature, from people in even the unlikeliest of places, from those we count on most, even from the mysteries.

Man may leave the barn to fall in disrepair, but God never leaves you. He always makes a way. Never ceasing to fill holes of sorrow and use a crack to bind souls in synchronicity. Sewing the tapestry of our lives ever interwoven in magic and mystery. His work of art that keeps us ever in wonder. What a grand design. Isn't that a way of Love?

Richness of Leaves

We live in a world where there's a plethora of leaves in all shapes and textures, colors and molds. There are an estimated 120 quadrillion leaves in the world.[2] Isn't it a wonder? So many leaves come from the same kind of tree. When they do, they don't just share these superficial features, they're fueled by common passions, common needs.

Leaves, like snowflakes, are so similar at a glance yet no two alike. So much the same in shape and size when they stem from familiar trees. The needled leaves of a pine tree thrive on acidic soil. Some, still, need the sudden sparks of fire now and then to begin again. Then there's the picturesque leaves of the maple that wither in acidic soil. Rather, they love the constancy of rain. People are the same sort of beings in a way.

---

[2] https://www.taranicholle.com/transformation-tuesday-the-lie-of-scarcity-%F0%9F%8C%BF/

Season's Change

It was a morning in mid-November, when the birds had flown south and the trees were mostly bare, awaiting the natural process of winter that loomed ahead. Something was different. I stepped outside and walked down to the lake. Across all its surface, as far as the eye could see, there was a swirling glaze of ice, as if Jack Frost himself had locked the water in time.

When I looked out on the lake, I understood something about life's process. About the time between life's seasons. Change is jarring. There are moments in our lives when change comes more suddenly than we can take in. Moments that etch themselves into our memory as something that shifted our reality forever. They happen to all of us. With death, birth, loss, meetings, heartbreaks, courageous steps, accomplishments, and decisions. So many aspects of life really can profoundly change in an instant, so much that I realize change is one dependable part of life.

In these moments, like a lake touched with the breath of winter, we may freeze. Locked in time as we try to comprehend them, absorb how they make us feel, understand what they mean for the past and the future and the now. Allow yourself time and grace. Because when life shifts and change jolts us, both positive and negative, we all need time to integrate it deep within, feel all the swirls of our emotions, let our new reality sink in beyond the surface of our hearts, reconnect to who we are amidst this new version of living.

Mind, body, and spirit, you deserve to be honored with time and grace. With these simple gifts come the ability to process and accept, celebrate and integrate, where you've been and where we're headed. In them, may you give yourself the power to more fully step into your new season, most of all within yourself.

FALL

Spiderweb

I walk along a path, and on that path I'm unmistakably smacked in the forehead with the strong thread of a spider's web. Woven between the limbs of two trees, this web is taught, thick, and unwavering against the force of my step forward. I jump back, startled in surprise, I pause, reaching to find where it came from as I also duck backward as if it could harm me in some way. Silly it seems we fear these things that cannot harm us. But we do. It's easy to find a fellow fearer of arachnids.

For me, this web itself was a representation of over analysis. For me, this web that weathered unknowable forces, standing the tests of immeasurable time, was sent to me today as a symbol of how I embark on love. When I begin to love someone, I step down a beautiful path such as this one this very day. With ripened blackberry bushes that stain my fingers as I pick them in the sunlight and curling vines across the wisping tails of tall grasses. It's hot and steamy outside, but I don't seem to notice because I'm entranced with the beauty around me, taking it in. When I take a new person in, when I fully admire them for who they are, it's in this light.

Then, something happens. Something that touches one of those invisibly familiar nerves like we all have if we've loved before in any way. A thread of analysis streams across my mind and I'm halted from my path forward until I can make sense of it. Knowing the vast depth of my love and therefore, knowing the hallowed depth of my loss, and I fear returning where I've been. I *must* know this path is safe before I proceed. I analyze and think. I feel and turn inward. I spin my own web of thoughts and feelings around myself until I've ensnared my ability to understand where I began, where I am, and where I could end. I only know that my senses, my feelings, and my mind are tired. To the point, I need a break from my skin, rest. I hide in this solitary cocoon I've made for myself. Perhaps I'll come out, perhaps I'll move on sadly, gracefully. Nonetheless, this is no metamorphosis. It's a retrieval of something lost within.

The feeling that it's safe to love. The trust in my own heart to guide me. The awareness that, just like I did on this path, I can lift up the thread of web because I recognize it as well, as anyone would. It's not a trap but an element of nature. One that once I did touch it, move it to make way, I couldn't help but marvel at the fortitude with which this creature can create. I can create too by moving webs rather than spinning them around myself in worry.

To tread the web is to become ensnared, but to truly respect it and allow it to be is to coexist with elements of oneself.

Whispering Winds

If trees could whisper, it would be in the wind that softly surges across all the forest, shakes the pine needles and quivers the poplar leaves. It rustles their branches and softens my spirit as it moves my senses right to where they need to be.

The Sunsets' Painter

Blue brush strokes curl across the evening sky. Like God had just freshly placed them there for those who chose to look up. They calmed and breathed the peace of night into the vibrancy of the setting sun. As it fell in the west, a new radiance of gold burst into the world as if to say that yellow is not just a happy color; it's vibrant, renewing, and breathes life with its arrival.

This sunset tells me that with every sunset in life, each ending, each goodbye, there is the radiant promise of a golden new tomorrow, one that breathes life into us just like the rising sun. Sunsets and sunrises are equally colorful for a reason. For they are equally insightful times rich in the hues of new insights and growth inside and out of ourselves.

It has been said many times over many eras that every closing is an opening. When I look upon the peace-invoking brushstrokes of the incoming night sky, I see that with the ending of one day comes a sense of quiet resolve, of closure and rest.

Because goodbyes and closings can heal, a sense of sadness for the loss of letting go. Blue is peace, in the soul, its truth in the essence of looking back upon the whole picture of a beautiful masterpiece. It's awe.

Sometimes the color blue is understood this way. But when you look across your entire sky, the whole picture that God has painted for you, you understand the power of truth, accompanying the blessing of peace.

And that yellow and blue go hand in hand. Both as equally precious blessings from God. For He gifts you with the abiding understanding of truth. Aren't the arts of His skies beautiful? Their inspiring promise never cease to assure my waking soul.

Goldenrod

I changed the course of my life the day I chose to move. A million little choices on so many levels led me to here, to epiphany.

I take my drive surrounded by goldenrods. Summoning the end of summer and the beginning of fall, yet this time fall does not mean letting go. It means change, like the rising of the sun in the east, knowing that it's inevitable, faithful in its ways.

In essence, perhaps it does mean letting go, but in the most beautiful of ways. The shedding of old skins to make way for new. Ready to take on a whole new world of His creation.

PART II.
WINTER

Introduction

Winter is a season that's cold and dark yet fresh and sparkling.

When we enter a winter season in our lives, we may be facing a sense of dark times or cold to bear. It's when our faith is challenged the most- faith in God and in ourselves.

Why am I in these circumstances? Will I move beyond this? How do I see my way through? are all questions we might ask ourselves and God in our journey through the dark.

Perhaps the loss of a loved one cast you into a winter of grief. Maybe a change in your home has left you feeling lost and alone. Whatever your circumstance may be, whichever part of your life, whether your winter time is happening amongst the snow or on a bright sunny day, it is a hard time.

Winter causes us to hibernate in a sense. As we navigate the questions and feelings inside us, we are called to go within to find the answers we seek. And in that inward journey, what we discover may change the landscape of our lives. We'll find new imprints of the soul are made upon the heart when we seek its wisdom. Our relationship with God fortifies. We tackle the reality of our lives and dig deep to make it through. What we are doing in our winter season is tackling a life lesson that's going to teach us more about who we are, what we want and need, and most of all, what we're made of. On this often quiet journey of discovery, we experience moments of sparkling epiphany and fresh fortitude in the midst of our agony. Just like snowfall on a cold winter's night.

Whatever your winter may be, you can do this. Have faith in yourself and in this journey God is taking you on. By the end, your commitment, to your spirit and His, can bring you to places you haven't imagined. These winters in life have the power to embody the spring.

Swans and Ducks

As winter began, a new pair of visitors frequented our waters. Trumpeter swans. Equal in grace and refinement, the duo were never far apart, always awe-striking. We were summoned to the window to take in their presence, watching their long necks glide into the water for breakfast.

One of Mom's and my favorite movie scenes comes from a film called *Love Affair* when a very old Katherine Hepburn explains to Annette Benning the difference between ducks and swans. Her grandson, Warren Beatty, thought he was a duck. He even acted like a duck, dating around and never seeming settled. What he didn't see was that his restlessness came from the truth he'd yet to discover. That he was a monogamous, soulful swan. It took finding a fellow swan in Annette to see it in himself.

The magic and devotion cast across the water between these two birds made that favorite scene more real. And the rolls and rolls of circles that their rhythmic rocking sent out into the glassy water made me wonder if a love like that has a ripple effect on us all.

The Life Within a Tree

The rings of a tree are a snapshot of what it has experienced in its years of life. Plentiful years of growth and slim years of little rain when it barely survived. Those rings stay stored inside its trunk. A private memory of where it's been. The trials it's overcome, and if survived, made it stronger. That's what scientists term adaptation. But before adaptation comes persistence. Persistence in response to life's elements seems to be its greatest strength of all.

SEASONS OF THE SOUL

Whirling Winds

Looking out across the white field that was once a wavy lake, the rolling winds of snow spark the imagination. Something about their force. It feels like a herd of wild horses could surge right out of the plumes of rising snow into clear line of sight, bringing a deep breath of energy from toe to head. They weave around you and encompass you in a single stilling moment, every hoof beat drumming in your ears. You take in their earthy scent, the stirred-up dust that catches in their coat. The moment fills you. In that single moment, you're overcome with their drive and togetherness and you carry it with you like a gift. Honored with an awe in knowing that a force like this exists. And you get to experience it.

That's what I see when I look out upon the drifting winds of our wintery lake. The rolling, twisting, whipping, curling snow drifts blow through the skyline, one towering billow after another. Each snowflake, riding in the wind across the course as it blows. Every ice crystal shifting in sync. Like a sandstorm, a raging drift of fog upon a dreamy morning's dew. When we pause to watch it out our snug winter's window after a drifted driveway of snow has been moved, we appreciate the power of this force. To shift the wintry sands beneath our feet. As the foundations of our lifelines seem to slip, sometimes the dunes of winter snow that rest when nature's calmed place us in a new world grant a different view of our landscape than before the storm. And we realize that the ferocity of storms, the might of their winds are just the power we need to whip old comforts out from under us and replace them with a new sense. A lens we'd ne'er earned were it not for having weathered the storm.

Knowing that storms come in life to refine our circles, renew our foundations, strengthen us, helps us take in the beauty of the details. Gusts' ability to change course in the snap of a moment, the beauty of every billow as it floats its majestic way across the lake and settles somewhere onto its piling destination. The forces of nature are unbridled and ever changing. Their might strikes awe, especially when we pause to feel them working their force in our lives, honor how lucky we are to experience and be a part of something bigger, stronger, mighty, taking hand and saying this is the way. Waking up the next morning, in an instant, or perhaps slowly, that new world whirled just for you.

As the moon's glow begins to cast its light upon the fresh fallen hills and valleys, you can see the flakes high up in the sky. Blowing, churning. You wonder where they'll land.

WINTER

Making the Ice

Blue. Ice, when it first forms, still reveals the lake beneath its glazy surface. A frosty layer adding a stillness that hearkens mystery to parts unknown. Ice forms a boundary between these waters and man for five months of the year in this part of the world.

There are seasons meant for us to tuck in, restore, and take stock. Just like the water before me this winter, something about having less exposure to the world renews us. Brings us back to our very being at the best we are now.

Ice is the key. In any season. For ice can be useful within a person in spring, summer, winter, or fall. It allows us the blockade between ourselves and those who need and want and use us so that we can be useful and wanted and needed by ourselves. So we can be still. And at peace. Blue.

Blue is also the color of truth. And there's a great power of release in facing it.

Owl

An owl came to visit me tonight. Beautiful, graceful, silent in flight. Her eyes penetrated my essence with their intensity. Sparking fear by propensity. The longer she looked, the more deeply it felt she was probing into the core of me, my spirit. I trusted her by nature, but she didn't ask first. She was already there.

I chased her away, afraid of her. In all her majesty and grace, she hesitated, looked at me. I told her once more. She turned and flew away, white in her wings. The guilt and regret never left my heart as I was telling her to go, for I loved owls. I trusted them. But with her I'd felt uncertain. It was the darkness of those eyes, deep and dark as the night. The way they dove into my soul without asking.

Friends asked first, didn't they? Maybe she was helping. She'd tried twice.

An owl's eyes are dark saucers for a purpose. They serve to see through the night. The thought lingered with me as I went about my day.

When the owl looked into my soul, she'd asked me, *Wherein lies your darkness?*... so that it may be brought to light. Not to be eradicated, but to be aware. Isn't that what bringing to light means?

Thankful for this prompting, I have the courage to see into myself now, to view with open eyes, to bring darkness into light. I won't a detail, for it's by diving into these spaces, that I can live open, true, and free.

Light to Dark

    I sat in the sun, taking in the comfort of its warmth like a cat. It felt extra good today, like I had more of it. I looked down at my lap. I had black pants on. The rays of the golden sun glowed into the black legs that soaked them in eagerly. The realization dawned on me that just as we so readily accept that dark is attracted to light, victimizing the good in the world, the light is attracted to dark just the same. We don't acknowledge that fact as readily, but it's true.

    A magnetism exists at a base level of our being that repels and attracts for the purpose of meeting the muse, the anterior prose of the self's opposite form. There's a cathartic effect for the soul to address and confront the inner issues at the depth of the soul that grind at the core of the inner essence. These meetings of light and dark bring about change that nothing else can stimulate. It's why these confrontations are necessary between others and within the self. There's a reason for the magnetism and a product of the pain.

Spiritually, light desires to fill the void, to warm it. Dark wants the void to be filled, to bask in its warmth. What we lack in understanding is that light and dark do not convert. There is a critical crossroads within the soul in choosing light or dark within. Once the choice is made, the meeting of light to dark is not a matter of conversion. It's a matter of confrontation. When they meet, when the light graces the dark, the dark takes sick delights of gains. The light gains hope for resilience, for change, until once again, it realizes that the dark is what it was and will be. Boundaries are important. They are not to be crossed. And yet why do we so desire to cross them? Why is the temptation there to try? Is the desire of the light to bring the dark to the brighter side, or is it something to be hidden, done away with?

Product of the pain. . . . When we confront the light to dark within ourselves, we can begin to catapult ourselves into manifesting our dreams. Because that's when we truly know ourselves. To know each angle and acknowledge it in its full form is to be able to dimensionalize the full body of your soul and use it to manifest your success for yourself and the world. It's not about conquering, control, or force. It's not about avoidance or shame or guilt. It's about the looking glass. Our inner eye where only we can see and know. It's about molding the body of our belief system to know that God made us to be a model of Him. And if we have flaws, those are meant to be worked through and with for the common good for us and His people. Not to be denied and choked. Flaws are beautiful. Because there can be so much magnificent beauty in the dark when we look past its maleficence.

What is my void? Wherein lies the darkness? What shall I bask in light to be warmed so that I may comfort what lies in the pain of void? Can you feel the warmth when you do? I still must focus to feel it there, in the wound, in that dark voided space. But I acknowledge I have that dark. I see that there's magnificent beauty in my dark through the way I can use it to truly see others, see through their dark, help them see through it too and further empower their light. I know too that my dark can be maleficence turned inward. Where does the pain originate? I know mine. Do you know yours? Therein lies the power.

SEASONS OF THE SOUL

Burls

Burls. From the outside, burls are not much to look at: large bulging knots in a tree. But from within, they appear as rich colorful swirls that create beauty within. Burls are so sought after by people that when seen on a tree in the woods, a man may cut down the tree and strap it to the top of his car to take home for the makings of a work of art. For some, a table, others a coaster, a sign, anything to be admired. It's a source of awe, inspiration, and admiration.

I see two burls on my way to work each morning. They hold up the mailbox of a home on the highway. Each time I pass it by and notice, I think of the cost. When we admire the inner beauty of these burls, do we ever truly know the painful process a tree goes through to attain it? How a beetle bores into its healthy trunk to tunnel through its insides, creating complex tunnels and designs only the beetle knows, maybe the tree. That the tree struggles to grow and bulges under stress in all its dying, trying effort to overcome, to heal and mend.

But we admire the damage. We see it as a trophy. Why is that? If we really knew what it went through to get that beauty within, would we see it the same way? Or is it our ignorance that makes our believe so. I hope that knowledge would change our perspective. Or at the very least, honor it in a more reverent, merciful way. Because mercy on a tree who's tried so hard is something I believe it deserves above all others. For it has triumphed above all. The burl tells me so.

Burls exist only in some people. Like their presence on a tree, they appear in the same color as the rest of its form. At times, they show as an ugly growth on the trunk. Most people pass it by with a curl of the lip, the recognition of something ugly, a deformity, something natural but not.

Burls exist in those who have had an infestation into their hearts. One they've had to overcome, much like this tree. Their bark and color does not differ from the rest, just like the tree. They've had to twist and compress inside, creating new colors and forms inside richer than one could imagine, just like the tree. They have overcome and live healthily, just like the tree. Some are judged for their ugly bulge, just like the tree. Others are recognized for the magnificent beauty that lies beneath the bulging, seemingly normal surface because they know what's inside, just like the tree. Some are used for it, just like the tree.

But unlike the tree, inside a person that beauty, the rich swirls of color, is an explosion of passion. A passion that when channeled rightfully created the beauty and change we need so desperately and most of all in this world. The kind of passion that touches the soul of another because it taps into the deep. Because the density of the fiber of the burl is representative of the depth of heart, the capacity for love and feeling that one has for being human. That only comes from walking the hard road over ashes of destruction within wounds of heartache overcome inside the bark. Confined inside the outer walls of normalcy until the right time and condition comes to express the true beauty that lies within. The true nature of the burl is an inner passion and depth and self-creation that comes from inner torture harnessed and channeled into light and love and something greater than oneself. Something that can change the world for someone else. Something for those passersby who can recognize the beauty in the burl.

Oaks

The energy of oaks is gentle, nurturing. The pathways of their branches tell a torrid story, yet it's not only one of their own. It's a thousand stories, the making of others whom its many branches reach out to. Each one bends and reaches, carving life into its way. Can you see it flowing through when you look up into the highest stories or across its winding bark?

The oak tree is viewed as wise and old. It has, indeed, stories to tell you. But most of all, if you listen, if you look, when you release yourself and *feel*, it has ever-flowing love.

Love that abounds for the journey of the trepid, with branches so long they rival its lofty height to reach into the corners of inward coves. With jagged branches, the tree mirrors their every breath in rhythm but reaches them, by love, in rhyme. By love, the oak brings safeness to those places only visible by the eyes of the heart, seeing the brilliant beauty of the soul.

The oak tree reaches the addicts enabled, for their way is the narrow branch that can break at the end. The oak is plentiful, and even narrow paths make way. Carefully, straightly, with a clarity only brought by the will-filled force of love. These branches are straight. They are possible. They are a way carved through thin air by the reaches of the old oak. Reach because you can, by the will of love, by the force of nature that is this tree in you.

New shoots filled with broad leaves begin at the oak's thick, established trunk. The oak will reach to anyone from anywhere. There is no matter of time or place. Love knows not of any importance of these things. It knows only of flowing, touching, pouring, filling, rising to the top of no ordinary way.

The oak's trunk shows places where something happened. A knot or the smooth circumference of what was once a limb, marking something missing. For a reason we may never know; a story untold, this notable mark is left for those who go missing because it's the only way to begin again. Can you feel it? If that mark is made by you, you are understood. You've left not just a story, but a mark that doesn't fade. A mark that's truly an essence that remains woven into this space. It will not be replaced but remembered. Begin again, new one, same one. You're felt deeply, always. Always you are deeply loved.

Some long branches curve down nearly to the ground, reaching those who've grown weary. With this flow of love, feel it's okay to fall down, but it's safe to stand back up again, to renew. If this fallen one is you, may you recognize the wonder of the moment when that branch reaches out in the most ordinary yet extraordinary way. For the breath of life this kind of love brings you fuels you to reach up, stand, keep looking, and live again, anew. You'll find a new reality has been made for you by that reach if only you say *yes* to love. Love creates the way.

Its branches spiral for those who twist too; you know if those are you. You are loved too, ne'er to be counted out for sake of sin. In every curl comes a story. And yet tree bark does not tell a soul. The things you have done, thoughts you've entertained, the energy you've conceived. . . . Know that in your soul, you are far, far more than these things. And that is why you're here. The oak tree knows this too. Do you? The branches holding twists and curls begin and end in a very different manner. Consider it, for this, truly, is the essence of you.

There's a place in the tree's trunk left hollow. The oak knows one someone everywhere who is searching, searching, searching for what is only found within. Yes, its heartbeat reaches there too. And when it does, if that searching one is you, you'll learn that peace, surrender, trust, faith, hope, unity, and love, love most of all, are accepted in the same vital breath of living. Living from within and beyond and again. With every deeper dive into the cavity that is yours on this tree, may you at once feel less solitary for your differences from those with branches and more unified with all that is. For you are one who shows others to find their way, who shines the way for more than you humbly imagine. Live beauty. You bequeath it.

Unmistakably, some branches lose their life force. They remain an echo of what was once there, a journeyed path to somewhere. For all things come and die. That is the circle. But to be loved remains always, so the branches remain. A memory etched across the skyline. Each one strongly outlined there so you too may know the echoes of their love still reverberate across the forest and far beyond the reaches of imagination.

The oak tree's love abides by the pure of heart who give without seeking, who see with knowing, who walk journeys only told between the whispers of its broad storied leaves. These are the beloved whom the oak knows will keep its own stories. For some of these folk exchange whispers with the tree on a breath of common vein. Not love in vain but the vein of unconditional love.

Vines lobby up its limbs, existing. Long there with the tree, some drape down in an artful, mesmerizing show of what can be when two exist as one song. Neither harm nor perish, rather they enhance one another's majesty. They are a show of the wisdom of allowance, of sharing. These two beings, the oak and the vine, so plainly they showcase the beauty in the multiplicity of love.

Bark that cracks and twists creates visions for my imagination. We can see a little bit of ourselves alongside every soul who's walked the Earth in the caricatured bark of these wise old oaks. It's like they're watching us right back. I invite you to open your senses; let them tell their stories. You'll find that every soul is a unique expression of love in its special form. Meant to be that way so that we can see the vast array of colors in the visionary landscape of love. Like the unlimited colors cast within a rainbow. What an adventure to discover the dimensions of what they look like, who they are, how they've been. Visions of love, touched by branches.

The old oak tree stands as a gentle pillar for us all. Everyone with purpose en-veined beneath the surface. The curvatures in its way, as each branch forms a musical rhythm of growing, form a heartbeat. One that flows out for the world of those that curve and bend, twist and narrow, break and fall low, rise up and move on. In essence, all of us. For in these things, aren't there elements of us all? And when we look at the rhythm and rhyme of the old oak's arms and skin, reaching, flowing, you can feel it. The unconditional love, the beauty, the formidable majesty that lies in the pure and deepest heartbeats of us all.

If you take the chance to spend some time with God among the oaks, *sense* this omnipotent presence, you can feel that the echoes of life and love live through these roots, reaching out to you. Humanity's roots. I invite you to let them tell their stories of how they were, as they reach and extend the pieces of their souls, still here in spirit. Perhaps you'll find in the casting rays of evening sunlight an echo that resonates your song. A connection. Soulsmeet. And when they do, what do you feel?

Rocks

"Why do rocks matter? Why do we care about knowing anything about rocks? You walk on them. They're a part of the dirt. WHY?" said the smartest boy in my class that school year. This was one of those moments when I wished I could share my faith with what I knew was an already faith-based student. I went there more times than were safe, but this would be too far. Here is what I wanted to say.

Everything in this world is a reflection of our Creator and all the beautiful meaning He placed there. Admired or disdained, each serves a higher need for our human survival and our spiritual creed. This kingdom is His gift to us. To lean into, grow in, and if we choose to allow it, through which to draw closer to Him. Think about how a geode cracks open as if revealing the magnificent beauty that lies within one's soul.

There's a rock, called the Petoskey Stone, which lies on a beach, gray like any other rock until the water touches it, revealing the imprint of the shining sun. According to legend, long ago, people spoke of the Petoskey Stone's magic. It was said that the little sunshine patterns that were revealed when water touched its surface symbolized the truth that there will always be a sun rising on a new day in the place you love most with the people you love most. To me, this means that love knows not the bounds of space and time. For once there, it is always with you, shining like the sun of a new day. It says to me also that sometimes, we need some waves to wash over our lives in order to reveal the beauty and wisdom that lies within us, to know that it's always there, to have faith in ourselves, to have faith in all of life.

SEASONS OF THE SOUL

Breaking Through the Poles

I wonder sometimes if narcissists and empaths come from the same home base. If they stare at one another as a mirror reflecting back the alternative of a choice they made in a pivotal time at the root of the soul. When faced with trauma, a choice is made: to dig in and know thy strength, to feel everything intensely; or else to stop believing and to spiral intensely away from compassion and love. Trauma is an extreme that sends out ripples, triggers, tremors. It permeates the senses of those around it. The souls affected can't help but respond. Once they do, their paths are changed forever.

When an extreme is experienced once, twice, three times, for years, in any forms, as if by Newton's Laws, it creates an equal and opposite reaction. Extreme. However, therein lies the choice within the soul, within the creatures that we are. Which way shall we turn? To feel or not to feel? To face or flee? To turn outward or inward?

Society tells us being stoic is brave. My beliefs are opposite. In my eyes, feeling is the bravest choice of all. When you feel, especially if you feel deeply, you know the humility it takes to identify emotions and face them. You know the courage required to let them flow and the power it takes to attend to them. Character is required for emotion.

To feel is to risk the greatest pains humanity has to offer, yet it's a multitude of other emotions that are so rewarding too. Joy, compassion, warmth . . . the ability to give and receive love.

In the face of extremes, some choose the courage of feeling through the extremes they're presented with. There is an intensity that comes with this choice that only someone who has experienced such extremes can relate to. Feeling the intent of harm on them, feeling the intensity of another. It creates a need, a need for heightened senses, not only for the protection of their bravely felt emotions, but a need to read their surroundings for mental, emotional, spiritual, and/or physical survival. This choice to feel creates a superhuman person who feels *more*.

A strong person has emotion and the character that is required to intentionally grow alongside it. They use these senses for compassion.

When someone chooses to turn away from feeling, what they foster is a belief in scarcity. It doesn't seem that character can exist without emotion. They use their heightened senses for selfish devices.

Sometimes, I wonder if the reason narcissists and empaths are so attracted to each other is that, at a spiritual level, they're drawn to their shared intensity and exploring the other choice.

Three Birds

There's something so poignant about the way a trio of birds flies through the air. It says that they care for one another. That when one bird loses his mate, a pair devoted solely to each other has room to take him under their wing. An act of equal respect and trust. Be it primal instincts for survival or a capacity for compassion, I think the birds show us a measure of humanity that's worth looking up to.

Tilted Trees

There are four trees standing very tall in the forest. My pass crosses under them as I walk along my favorite way. They allure me with their anomaly. For in the ground they grow from is a steep unforgiving slant of erosion. The kind that surpasses the speed of growth so that all four individuals are left tall, straight arrows pointing diagonally across the sky. So much so that if it weren't for each other, they would not stand. They would fall and succumb to death. But each pine and birch in this foursome is very much alive and thriving. These living creatures give life to one another through the fortune of geography and timing. So together they remain tall, straight, and strong with a reciprocal needing of each other. There's beauty in the way their branches intertwine. It makes you feel special as you walk in witness of them beneath their pointed archway. Wedding arch.

In truth, nature can be harsh in its elements, but there is an artful grace in the needing of things for each other and a magic in the way that grace gives them life. People are much the same as these trees. And so is the magic of love. Lean into your grace gifts where life and love prevail.

Ice Shards

At the start of winter, ice glazes over the lakes. At the start of the cold, a thin crust forms to encase it until the right conditions strike. Perhaps a warming, then a brisk winter wind, just enough to crack that ice into hundreds of shards and little sheets that lap up on the western shore. The sound of ice crystals pummeling against one another captivates the spirit, calms yet enlivens the mind with a still sense of wonder. You reach out to touch them and marvel at how delicate this large and majestic process really is. And a knowing settles within you: once this ice settles, this crust rhythmically built, solidified, sculpted with shards and broken pieces, it will be a layer far stronger than that which came before.

Beauty Illuminated

Embers of pale yellow give rise to lime green that melt into blue from a light that draws the blend of colors up to touch a midnight black sky. And as if with the tap of one finger, the light of dawn's rising sun sends a surge of deep blue across the vast, starry sky.

As those colors touch night into day, our effervescent stars are mysteriously hidden until night allows them to light our way again. But a few of the brightest remain for hours. They shine as intently as ever before. They remind me that stars never leave us. The magic feeling they give me when I gaze up at them of a night can be found if only I remember they are there. Seen or not, they are with me, guiding in the night, holding fast in the day. Just as the sun's world holds us in reverse.

Dawn's Light

The dawn's light against the coal black silhouettes of tall pine forests move the spirit. They show a different point of view of these strong and steady creatures that have stood much longer than I. The glowing backdrop magnifies every contour of their sculpted journey, how they've been cast from the wind, toward the sun and the rain. When we pause a moment, we feel the magic, knowing they're a little like us all.

PART III.
SPRING

Introduction

Springtime is when we stretch into all the discoveries we made through the dark. We come to realize the opportunities being born from life's trials. With courage, we step forward by trying new ways on new feet. We grow beyond where we've been. We courageously greet the sun despite the still residual bouts of cold that snaps the air.

When you have evolved in some aspect of yourself, the natural next step is to integrate that growth into your life. This takes practice, persistence, and bravery. You are coming into your own again. Believe in you. Allow yourself to stumble but keep going. This process is directed by the will of your spirit, the intentions of your soul, and the love of God for the world. You have something new to bring forth to it. This is going to be scary but delightful, challenging yet self-affirming, slow and steady, within and without. Root deep, spring forth, and blossom.

Inherent

I came upon a baby deer curled up in the grass. She still looked wet, and her eyes still had that hazy blue. She wasn't startled at all by my presence. I kept a respectful distance from her as I watched in awe. She lifted her little head and smelled the air around her, touching the grass with her nose. Her lip lifted with each sniff. The sun was bright and warm. Then, she decided to stand. She put her legs underneath her and took her first steady steps, her legs almost unnoticeably quivering as the thin fawn made her way toward the safe forest. What a gift to watch her very first steps! She was sure. She knew her way. She was following her instincts.

Mysterious Journey

When I bike, my favorite route to take is a route unknown. Turning down a road I've never been and seeing where it takes me. If the route turns out like the one I chose yesterday, those roads lead to fields of wildflowers, where the pavement turns to gravel and my tires stir up hundreds of tiny butterflies that softly brush my sunkissed arms, bringing a pure smile to my face as they burst into the illuminating skyline, drawing my focus up to the gentle sounds of joyous songbirds and the beautiful face of a doe standing just yards before me as she peacefully ponders disappearing into the forest once again. Rides like these feed the soul, filled with the awe of what I view as loving gifts from above. There's a challenge in pushing against the wind up the inclines of the hills, making me dig deep for strength and endurance, but the discovery that lies at every peak and valley of those hills makes that challenge satisfying, fueling, breathtaking.

Other rides down these mysterious roads are less romantic. They may have inviting wildflowers and a long and winding lane, but as I enter, a feeling of disillusionment already settles somewhere in my consciousness. I proceed with curious optimism. As I travel down this road, the beauty of the landscape draws me in. I travel farther seeing where it leads until I find myself assaulted by a fly, then another and another until I realize I must ride full speed to ward off full on attack. Suddenly, the beautiful road ends in the form of a rouge metal gate with remnants of a padlock hanging off, rusted old chain. Beyond that, thick woods. I turn my bike around while simultaneously thwarting off my small following and proceed back to the main road to return home. I don't regret going down this road. It was pretty for a while, but as my instinct told me, there were things hiding in those beautiful flowers that could pack a bite and the path led to an eerie dead end. All is fair in the game of country roads. It's part of the adventure.

Both of these experiences are completely real, every minute detail, but they struck me as metaphoric of navigating the pathways to love. On the wrong road, that off gut feeling is the first sign followed by some beauty which is a very brief illusion. Then the flies are the warning signs that multiply and nag you though you may proceed, telling you something isn't right and will hurt you. The padlock, perhaps a lock on someone's heart. The dead end, just that. In contrast, the right road has the butterflies. Those butterflies are the little moments when a person makes you feel alive, inspired, touched, cared for in a new and real way. The little things they say and do that bring an infectious smile to your face. The songbirds like the sound of their voice and their words that speak to both your mind and your heart. The doe, someone's vulnerability, so beautifully revealing themselves to you in full form amazingly, touchingly with little trepidation. This road goes on and on. Over time, it becomes a little less exhilarating but rather calming and comforting with moments of surprise as I ride along, something I find equally fulfilling and also metaphoric of time spent in love. The wind and hills represent the fact that this beautiful awe-inspiring road isn't easy.

It takes hard work and effort, and commitment. Without that, those discoveries would not be made, and the beauty of that road and its journey would be lost.

Which road are we, I wonder to myself? Are we a road of tiny butterflies? Or are we one that has a gate at the end? I keep both hands on my handlebars and breathe in each discovery, keeping my senses open. And as I take each day as it comes, I enjoy the ride down this road with my friend.

Thunder

You go about life's doings, just as you've always done. Just as the day goes. But suddenly, subtly, there's a growing sense of stillness. A stillness merged with urgency that presses you forward. Something must be done, lest it will be tucked away. You'll be tucked inside until the storm is over. What do you need to prepare? What have you wanted to be done? A storm brings its lightning bolt of checking in with our own reality. Am I where I need to be, with whom, and why? Isn't it nice to have such a check with our reality to remain close to what life means?

A married couple once adopted a dog. They chose a shelter dog because second chances were in their hearts. When they brought a pitbull home, he was afraid of men, including the husband.

Ray was gentle with Sammy's fears, with a saddened understanding of how fears are planted. Their hearts understood one another, and Ray's had the power to heal Sammy's.

With gentle guidance, Ray showed Sammy that love is safe from a man—from this man. Because it was. It was a love to rest in and rely on. To play with and find home in.

In the world, it was Ray's presence that made others feel looked after, safe. And it was his actions too. Ray made an effort with people whom he knew went unnoticed or misunderstood. He made them smile, laugh, feel equal. He was the man who noticed a woman's car against a utility pole. He was the man who leapt from his own truck and right down the highway to warn her of draping power lines. He was my brother who held my world still when I lost a friend on an early Sunday morning. For Sammy, he was the man who gently carried Sammy's large frame down the basement steps when the tornado siren alarmed and Sammy was trembling in fear. Ray was the man who held him there and whispered to him softly to erase the memories of other lives in other basements until all he could feel was Ray's love. Feel the truth that he was safe, home.

For finding these truths in Ray, Sammy was able to step fully into the truth of who he was. A healer clothed in fur. For comfort, empathy, safety, play, being there. . . . They're all given in reciprocity when two hearts recognize their equal capacity. They fuel each other.

In this home, Sammy healed others through his eyes. Eyes that gazed with wells of caring. Through a presence that was ever aware of the pulse of people's hearts as they beat with more than blood. Sammy healed for being there, laying across a lap, standing near, a language that words wouldn't justify if they could have been shared.

Ray came to find in Sammy the same home that Sammy found in him. At the end of tired workdays, on the cusp of quiet losses, when feelings need not be articulated, only shared through the air. What was shared between this man and his dog was an uncommon depth of caring, of feeling, of knowing the world at its best and its worst and traversing it. I believe that similar souls find each other this way as a gift of growing through it. As one of the ways God shows us He sees.

A man and his dog can be a strong bond, but beyond that, this man and his dog shared largely beating hearts that went out to others in profound yet quiet ways. Sometimes, it's those unknown healers of the world who are felt most deeply. They leave a mark on you. And it's the kind of mark that settles in with a knowing that the world is a little safer, softer with them here. Showing that beyond all strong exteriors, loving grace and gentleness are the truest measures of power and strength.

Storms. There's no exception to their ferocity. When they come in, they're a force of true nature. Calm preparation gives way to an enormous release of power, fury . . . energy. I know you can feel it too. Don't be afraid. Energy is released into the world so that it can be made anew. That's what this storm is doing too. Let it guide you. The same fury that makes you feel alive, feel fear, is the same force that, as it passes, washes everything anew. Let the pouring rains run down every sense of you. But only after you've raged, you've sobbed, you've worried, you've weakened, you've turned your back on yourself. Because the release of those bolts of pain electrify you with a light unknown before they struck your sky. The thunder of your fists quake your world into shape. Be the storm. But let it pass. For it too could define you.

Let the rains that follow shower you with a knowing that all is safe again. All is calm. Fair. Known somewhere. And when the rain stops, open your eyes. Wipe the drops from your face. Look around you. There's a force still. A new one. . . . Color everywhere. Color in the rainbow, cast against the gloom. Color in the clouds as the sun sets. Color in the eyes of the man as he gazes out the window. Known. And color in his nanny dog's soul. Realized.

Soul Growth

The sound of the wind in the treetops give me the feeling of a home all my own, one to be shared with the creatures of the woods, like the chickadees that chatter joyfully behind me as I settle down in the moss by the stream. The twinkling leaves tell me that there are few of them left in this part of the forest come fall, but those that remain have found a new freedom to wobble and *move*. The peat moss and the tree roots, the twigs and the needles, soften my steps as the trickling water breathes life through its sound from below.

Below, at the forest floor, the landscape draws the senses, like traveling to a different land. To a place that, when you are closely present with it, is filled with sounds and smells, rich in colors and meaning.

When I reach out to touch the earth, peat moss gives way underfoot. Though still alive, it is hinting at the transformation taking place beneath my feet. In that moment, I realize that everything around me, this very moment, is temporary. The beauty of my surroundings is a masterpiece not quite ever complete in its formation. Within its overturning process is where unending progress and beauty lie.

Everyone has special places they call their own, those they return to in winter, summer, spring, or fall. Perhaps a certain tree caught their attention or the formation of a rock. Maybe the glass surface of the special pond where a little girl caught frogs each summer until nature took it back into a stream once again. Nature has a way of making things new again. Different, changing, morphing: they're all one and the same, yet natural. To a particulate level, decompositional change is ready to form something else entirely, yet always bringing them back to their purest form, wild, free.

This process, my memory of the pond, this moment here in the moss by the clear water stream, they all say that to love a place is not to own that place. For it too has a majestic cycle underway, not unlike our own. Through a broader view of life and death, this forest with its trees and peat moss, are each part of a grander picture. It has a rich journey to carry on, far greater than we may perceive in a moment or even a lifetime. The same can be said for the love of one person.

Yet it still says more. The little hills that give this forest floor its character, covered in rich green moss that shines in the sun, are gifts from a tree gone by. Perhaps fallen in a winter storm or tumbled on a windy day like today. Many years ago, that tree gave new life to the beautiful landscape I see right now. It made me realize this truth:

The beauty right here that touches my heart was built on the beauty of yesterday. And that on which came before. Each enriched by its predecessor. In that understanding, I come to see Gods works a little more clearly.

The magic of tomorrow is built upon the love of yesterday. Nothing is ever lost. A life that passes will be infused and redefined into the life that comes next. When you embrace the experiences, the senses, and wonder of life's cycles, your heart will always be filled with home.

Swallowtail

A swallowtail struggled into view, showing me the cadence of its droughting efforts. I leapt to the ground as my heart followed. Stepping swiftly onto my hand, I saw a soul in need, a single broken wing. Enveloped in my sheltering hand, now protected from the forceful wind, his struggling ceased. His relief in resting touched me for, suddenly, his world was better, easier. I felt the spark in his heart and the tired weariness in his spirit. I embraced him with all my love. For every creature, no matter how small, finds these tumults in life.

As he rested in the embrace of my sheltering hand around him, blocking him from the unrelenting wind, my thoughts suddenly surrounded him too. My thoughts were nothing but protecting him from harm, fixing that wing, wanting so much for him to fly again so he could be free, golden in his spirit.

I wanted so badly for there to be a way for me to fix his wing, help him fly, be whole and free again. I thought about what placing this creature on my hummingbird feeder would do. It would make him vulnerable to birds. A flower would be best in this wind. But what settled in my heart was a sadness for him. He wasn't going to fly again, feel the freedom of his wings. I wished it wasn't so. But I had to let go of that desire in my heart for him; I had to accept his truth. Healing him was not in my power. What was in my hands was the simple ability to make his time in this world better, easier, more loved.

I saw broken wings all around me, but it wasn't my job to fix all broken wings. Somehow this need within me made me wonder, could there be broken wings in me, caged wings? If I were so inclined to find them and heal myself? Perhaps we all have them somewhere within us in places we don't heal ourselves. Isn't the nature of life a purpose for healing? So why can't I heal my butterfly? Why can't my sincerest heart's desire change his world? In some cases, an outside force can come in and cast a rainbow of change upon a cloudy sky. But the greatest power for healing in one's life rests within their own spirit and soul. Because the challenges we face in life are our own. They're ours to face, and ours to take. When we heal them within ourselves, we empower a spirit of evolution within our soul that no other can ignite nor perpetuate. Real change.

If we were to change and evolve on behalf of other's souls, we would deny them the feeling of earning their wings to fly on their own, in this life or beyond. They could never know what it means to deepen their faith through struggle, triumph over trial. It is through facing our most harrowing trials and hollowing truths alone or beside someone that we become strong of mind and heart but even more, mature of spirit and soul. That is an essence of living that changing force for others cannot deny. It's a force of nature, a law of existence.

I'd tended and mended swallowtails in my life. They clung to the tenderness and joy I poured onto them just as he did on our walk together, finding shelter and love in their storm. But it took me years to absorb this lesson. The power of personal change. And once I did, I empowered not just my butterflies, but myself. Because no longer was I endowed to be their savior. I was entrusted to make their life a little better, more loved. For the lessons were theirs, and I had my own.

Life has a way of testing our wings. We have opportunities to heal ourselves, trials. With every pivotal trial, we are faced with the choice to fall into a hole of sorrow or remorse, resentment or hate, envy or listlessness. A multitude of darkness in these holes. Or we can reach up for that healing hand by the will that rests within our every soul.

Within every soul lies the will to persist. Within every soul lies the potential to overcome by hope, faith, love, acceptance, truth. But not in an airy sense that goes undirected and undefined. We must seek our soul, silence the noise outside and within to hear what our heart and soul is guiding us to. It's like God's voice and yours in cohesion guiding your way. Always a voice of Love. Stay ever in touch with this voice.

Consult this voice when you have wings that need mending. You'll still fall into the valley, but as you do, you'll see that valley helped you see all the truths you needed to appreciate the view when you come to the peaks. When the valleys of those broken swallowtail wings ache, when they feel like they'll never end, keep the faith. Faith is all that will keep you to the end. It's what will connect you to that abiding voice within that keeps you going, keeps you on the path to your own glory. Your light that shines ever-brightly. It is not dim, if only you can see it, hear it, know it is always there. With every healing wingbeat, you are growing. And when you fly, the pigments of every color in your wings will hold a depth of color that matches the new understandings built into your spirit from your pathway. Colors of compassion, empowerment, peace, understanding, a higher kind of love.

Though my desire to mend and fix may be strong, I know that I can only lend a helping hand, a guiding light. These journeys must be taken by oneself, not by someone else. The desire to fix is a disservice, for true power comes from healing oneself, and the deepest healing only happens from within. Honor each other as we honor ourselves. We share but don't carry.

As great gifts, we have the opportunity to bring healing to each other's hearts. But it is our personal duty to realize who has the potential to be touched, who can be inspired to heal themselves from the inside out, and who has chosen to remain broken. It's a law of honoring human will and of protecting your heart within. It helps me know that when I come across a set of wings that can't be fixed, my unending love for them is enough. It's enough to make their world more tender, more loved, more joyful, so that they may feel those things fly by happiness and love.

As I let go of my need to fix my swallowtail, I swallowed acceptance and thanked him. Knowing my love is enough was where my wings needed mending most of all.

SEASONS OF THE SOUL

The Storm

Ripples of change come like the clouds with the weather.

A storm is coming. Listen. Act. feel its energy course through you. It has something to tell you about your life. It will destruct. When it leaves, things will be broken and damaged you never thought would be. But as you sort the debris, you'll find those ripples cast an effect that reaches far and wide, reshaping and sculpting your present in a way that feels strange and your future in a new lens you've yet to fully hold. But let me tell you, the energy of that storm should not be feared. It is the very storm that makes anew. Honor the old, but look onward. Beautiful color touches the horizon if only we choose to see.

When it storms up here it feels as though the sky is closer than anywhere else on Earth. You feel it in your bones as a boom of thunder reverberates through your chest, clashes right over the cabin, echoes through the treetops. Is it possible that the sky could really be that close? That this thunder could crack just above your rooftop? You'll wonder until you're drawn to the window against your mother's will to see the piercing electric fingers of lightning stretch across the sky. Only for a moment. Leaving you lingering in awe at the pane holding your breath for one more rumble through your rib cage. It's like all that electricity charges the air and channels right through my spirit. I could think of no better way to start the day.

The rain pelted the window in drops that seemed to get larger by the moment, making this cabin I adore feel like a cozy haven. A small part of me, okay a big part of me, hoped the power would go out just so we could get out the lanterns and light the candles, nothing else but that warm glow. I went around the house and lit them, just to capture that feeling. And I just sat and took it in. Just like that, it was gone as quickly as it came, the hush of gentle rain chasing in its wake.

Pine Branches

New growth on a pine tree in spring is a lot like people. Starts out small and tender, a pale green that tinges in the heat of day and bends in the storms of night. But as it grows, the elements harden its needles to bear the storms. The very elements that challenge those newborn needles deepen its color so it collects the sun's energy as its own. They strengthen it into something that can withstand and even thrive in the brutal thirty-below winds of the northern winter skies. They prepare what's new and vulnerable for the tests of the Earth, so that, with the life of the tree, each one's beauty only deepens and grows.

There's no deeper dimension to the color green than pine needles shining in the setting sun. I look at them in wonder. That's what God has done for me. Mind, body, and soul.

Raindrops

In the forest it rains. But not all the water hits the ground at once. Some of it lingers in the leaves till morning. It waits to fall until the rays of the sun hit the morning dew. And then it's as if the weight of the world is unleashed from each branch. A gentle shower cascading down in a cacophony of water and air, the sound of a rainstorm on a sunny day.

Just like the aftermath of an inner storm. The raindrops sometimes wait to fall in their own appropriate time. When the sun is shining. When warmth from a new day touches it. When the world doesn't know where it's coming from. But the trees are releasing the cleansing weight of the world to shower the earth below with a bath of nourishing drops to grow from.

This kind of morning was the season of life I was in. Listening to the sound of those branches in the breeze, I understood this was another way of living. Best done from the soul.

Morning Air

As I walked along our road, the scents of vanilla, mint, cedar, and pine lingered in the woods from the nighttime air. They drifted out into the dawning day and permeated all my senses. The rich body of it filled more than just my lungs as I stepped onto the path. I felt the earth in every breath I took in. It filled my heart. The sun touched my skin and sent a shiver of warmth into a chill I didn't know I had.

Daytime is meant for the world, for activity and togetherness. Nighttime is for slumber, a time when we visit our deepest selves. On the cusp of these two is morning, where both conscious and unconscious meet. It's like a catch between two worlds. Asleep and awake, both within and without. The morning shows a magic on the cusp, when the world is quiet enough that we remember those parts of ourselves we only visit in our sleep. The natural wisdom and insights we can bring to the world are who we truly are at the soul, felt in the rising light by the quiet misty dew of the morning.

Paper Wasp

The process paper wasps go through making their nest is much like how a heart makes a home. First, they must find the perfect safe location to build from. For a wasp, a tree limb beneath the shade of leaves. For a heart, on the shoulder of one who will stay there. One who will see and feel and hear and love. Ardently. This takes discernment, some would say through experience. Others would look back upon the wasp and know there's a deeper instinct that drives us to our highest needs if we listen and let them.

Next comes the hard work. Once we have found that proper location to rest our hearts, build the home of our hearts, we must know that home needs walls. A safety net from the world around. Isn't that the great haven home is?

The paper wasp is a steady creature. Intent on building. The process by which a paper wasp retrieves mouthfuls of wood fibers to return them to their nest for homemaking is something of an art. They go out into the world and take something rough and soddened and transform it. They make it entirely new in preparation of a home. Creating soft pulp, their masses of work become delicate, intricate layers of a naturally made paper. Sheets that swirl with texture and curl around one another as a solid unit. A one-piece design made of a million fruitful labors. Labors of love.

The heart is much the same. A person goes out into the world and brings with them many hard, soddened experiences that can be transformed into something soft and new. Something worthy of building a life from, protecting a heart with. Wisdom, feelings, prayers, and dreams, whether they're one and the same or all in all, are meant to be shared steadily with care. They're the building of the nest. The walls that two can create around their hearts to protect and make a sweet haven from the world and nest within. Cherish each other more with every layer thin. For within the art of building, what's in those intricate walls is trust, respect, knowing, hearing, care, sincerity, hope, and dimensions of each other found between layers that no outside world may ever see or know but two can revere. You're building a home for two hearts to be safe in each other, enveloped by each other from the world. For within the art of building, what's in those intricate walls is the art of making love.

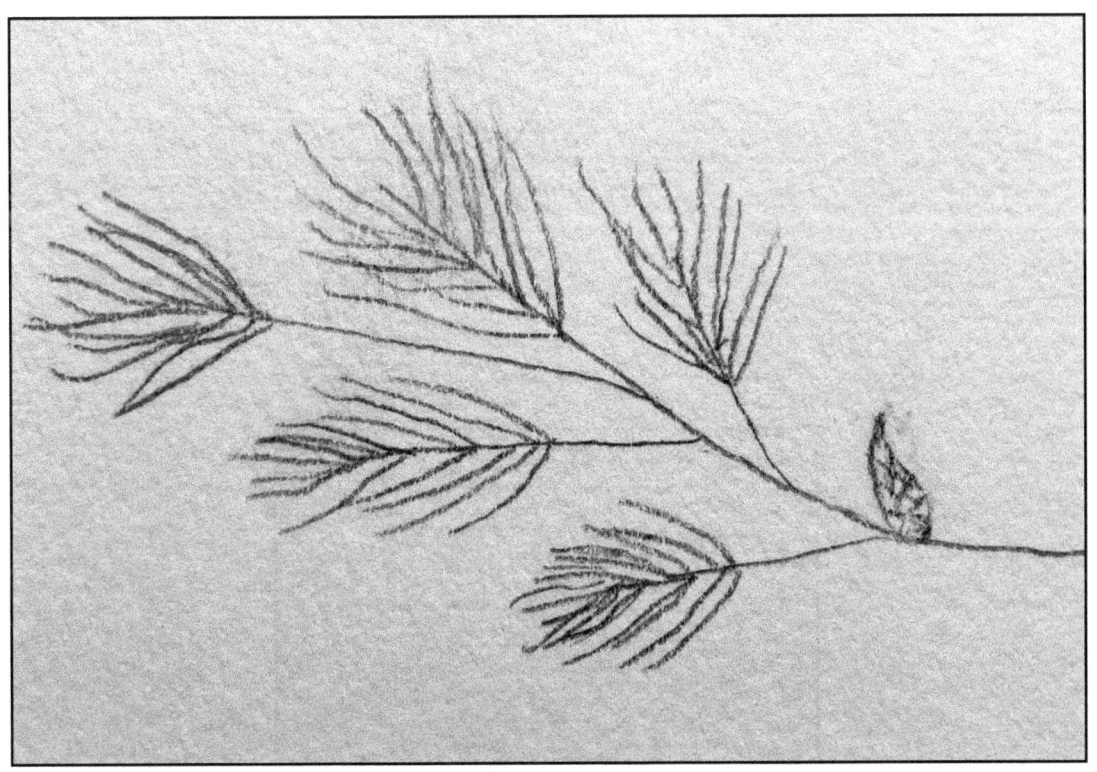

Jack Pine

Leaving abuse is like walking through fire. It takes courage to burst through the flames, but you know deep within that's the only way to go. Those flames burn you in many places as the culmination of an old life gone sears your skin. Family, friends, places, things, memories, plans, loss. But once you're through, the smoke clears. And you realize the fire burned what was needed. It was making way for the best yet to come. Your life's dreams.

There's a special tree that lies within these woods. It requires this very process to exist. It's called the jack pine. Its seed can lay dormant for twenty years poised for the moment when the way has been cleared for it to awaken from its slumber. When fire strikes, the old familiar forest is gone as if it never were, leaving char in its wake. And yet, in the sunshine springs the start of the tall, sturdy new growth of a tree who was made for this moment, who needed it to live. Who's basking in the light of its first pure rays of sun. The new growth of life that envelops around it will look never the same. And that may be the fiercest flame of all.

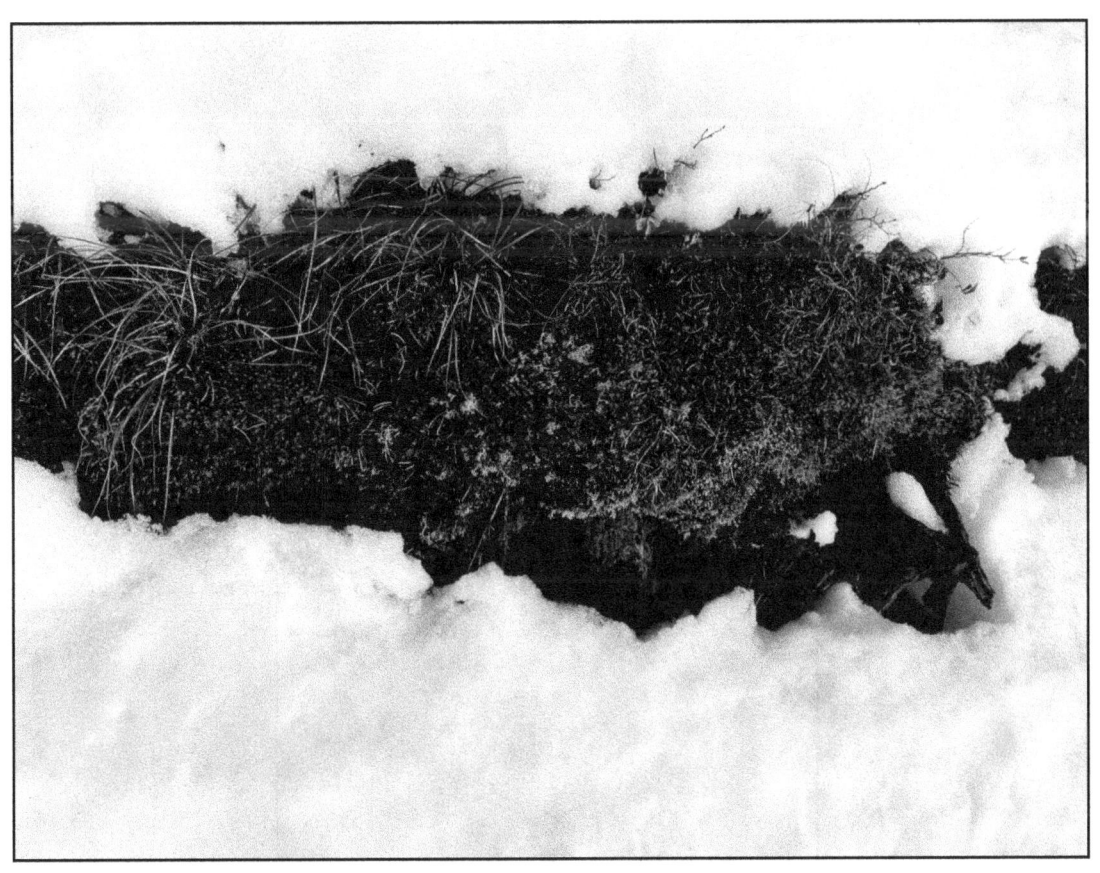

Effervescence

Snow. Layers upon layers of snow deepen over hills and valleys of the north-wooded Earth, encasing its life in frozen time. One would think under all that weight of water and time, all of life would be smashed. Some of it is. Grasslands flatten, ready to be composted into new. But other beings, like moss, lichen, wintergreen, and prairie willow, they spring forth the moment the sun strikes them once again, as if the tests of time, and yes snow, never touched them. Glory be to the plants who bear weight while being weightless; there's an effervescence to their springing that sings praise to us all. All who rise to greet the day upon the lifting of mighty weights.

A Rose Opportunity

Rose-colored skies come in pockets. They come in passing openings of light in the blanket of clouds that form the coming night.

You spy their reflection upon the lake below, a glowing hue of soft warmth upon the choppy waters. Their soft light calls to you for a reason. For in that open light lies an opportunity. An opportunity to feel the very same softness and warmth, gracefulness and kindness, care and touch to the heart, and most of all, above all, love. All these things, that are in you and that very sky, are telling you something.

The heavens above offer you the greatest love, the kind of love for you. It will come this same way and move your spirit this same way too. Will you say yes to it? The opportunity is fleeting, for life shows many forks in the road.

The clearing in the clouds that opens to this lovely rose light and feeling stays there for a little while. It allows me to take it in, to absorb all its meaning, for it holds so much. But opportunity comes as a hand outstretched to take. Will you take it?

This opening is a hand outstretched to take.

But in the moment, it starts clipping past as if to say that opportunity is just that. You must take it to hold because some of life's treasures are once, twice in a lifetime, beyond them a blanket of the dreams' slumber.

Love is something to grasp, to hold, to take on tightly and never let go. To say yes to when an opening comes in your sky. Because that love was brought, softly, warmly, gracefully, kindly, caringly, touchingly, in beautifully magnificent Love just for you. Take it. You deserve it. The hand of true love is reaching out to hold. Believe. You'll fly. . .

Climbing into Me

I made my way over hill after hill in the woods until I came upon a clearing. The wind blew my hair back from my face as the sun kissed my skin. A still, small voice asked me, "Well, are you going to pull yourself together and live your dream?"

I could sit in the sorrow of losses in life. I could hide in the fear of "What if?" I could run and ignore my inner knowing. But where would that lead besides a place on my path where I look back and feel I've not fully lived?

I could ignore the calling in my heart and follow the predictable path, yet that pathway made me smaller than I truly am, smaller than I could be, should be. It would take strength and bravery to enter the unknown my heart was leading me to. But the heart is where God and I meet, so to have faith in its stirrings seemed the only thing to do.

I'd felt the precipice of this choice for a while, but now it was time to choose: action or rest. It was time to have the confidence to recognize the signs great and small. They gift us in a plethora of anomalies sometimes hidden in our superficial world.

It was time for me to take the million little steps it took to make large change. To step fully into myself, to share me with the world without reservations. This means different things to all of us. Only we truly know our way. Listen in. Look within. You'll feel it too. Sometimes it takes exploration to parts unknown, but I promise you you'll find there a piece of you now shown.

I've noticed through the years that people who are dead inside have already given up on their dreams. It breaks something inside them. I did not want to live in that void.

I share with me and others a fuller kind of me. And in so doing, I honor the gifts God placed in me. It's our duty to look into the depths of our dreams. What they tell us will abound in wisdom and assurance for what we're set to do in life.

I say yes to every dream. Will, determination, and commitment replace fear. I believe in my dreams. They all lead me to discover myself, and they each hold power to bring my light to the world. What dream inside your heart is pulling you to unfold your light into the world? Follow it.

I follow the sunshine as it warms my entire body. The scent of the field was like an aromatherapy permeating my senses. I follow these feelings. Alive. And when I come to the other side, where the woods shelter me once again, I realize I've not really changed along the way, I've become.

PART IV.
SUMMER

Introduction

Summer is a time to relax into all the ways you've grown. Through your seasons of development, you have proven a lot to yourself. Most importantly, you've stayed true. Appreciate who you are now.

By blossoming into your new self, you find that life is never perfect, but it can be doubly fulfilling when we soak in precious moments.

Moments when long-time voids are filled in an instant.

Moments we realize the worth of our purposeful presence in someone's life and theirs in ours.

Moments we are thankful to God as we realize the alchemy and beauty in life's process, through all trials and pain.

It's by the depth of gratitude we embody in our summer seasons –for ourselves, for nature, the people who've touched us, and God- that we feel the warmth of the sun shining in our hearts.

Life won't always glow like this. Take it in. Always remember that to get here, life showed you the depth and vastness of your heart, your soul, your spirit. Through challenge, you've discovered your potential, and as life continually unfolds, the cycles of its seasons always begin again.

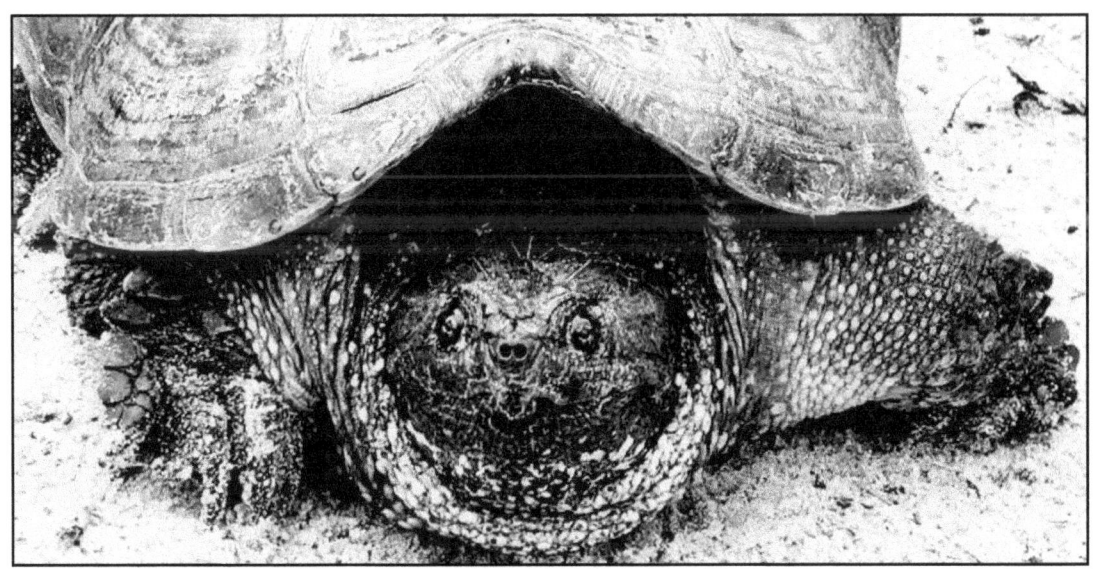

Basking

As I churned my paddle through the water round the bay, I spied a shape above its surface, not so far away. Curiosity lured me once again, and I followed it. A red painted turtle sat perched atop a log basking in the sunlight in a perfect picture of bliss. How could one deny the feeling so openly shown across this small creature's whole body? He was soaking in pure comfort and joy with every ray of sunshine he took in. At that moment, I noticed the chorus of frogs had begun once again since the departure of my stranger danger. It was a sound of happiness, no urgency or crying out for need, just "happy" that spilled into me. Hearing those frogs in their blissful, safe haven and watching that turtle basking in the sun, I realized something. Life is meant to be enjoyed with purpose. Sure, turtles sunbathe for body heat. It's a means of survival. The song of the frogs is their mating call. Without it, they would cease to exist. But, there is no denying that these small creatures were taking pure and utter joy in the necessary of their lives. And ought that be?

Eagle Angel

Walking down the road, I couldn't help but notice the majesty of the clouds in the clear blue sky. They towered and billowed, illuminated by the light of the brilliant sun beyond them. As I gazed upon them, I noticed something different. A small band of clouds. They weren't up highest, for the high clouds sat seemingly still at their peaks above. They weren't the lowest in the sky. Those low drifted south as the wind marched them away.

Nearly imperceptible, this small band of clouds, amidst yet so different from the rest, cast their own way north. It's what made me notice them. It was as if they were moving their own brave and brazen course across the sky. Drawn, I couldn't help but listen with every part of me, most of all my spirit.

Walking towards the dock, I nestled down into the reeds as I sat down on a low step that led down to the water. Those clouds were telling of the power that rests in taking courage to move your own way. They spoke of having the courage to honor oneself by leading thy own path. Of independent thought and listening to the soul's stirrings, quietly, gracefully different from the rest.

The shape of an eagle became clear in the heart of those clouds. Its eye, a powerful point under the strong curve of its head that was brimmed in a hue of cobalt blue. That blue traced down to a soft and lovely pink at the edges where its neck feathers would meet the body were it alive. It was as if the sun were casting colors into the light of that cloud with a mind of power and voice of love as if they were one and the same.

In awe, I watched, touched by the grace with which God sculpts even the smallest details of our skies. And in that awe, I saw a change morph through the form of that eagle as the wind drifted it into the shape of an angel. With blue arms like wings and a soft pink rimming the hems of its flowing skirts. The angel's beauty filled my heart with wonder and grace. Perhaps walking the path the soul leads grants us the most beautiful moments of wonder and love. A pure gift for sure.

I watched until the forms were gone.

Song of Silence

I set forth on my paddle board. The intimacy of being alone with nature made all of my senses relax into reverie as I cast out upon the lake. Where would I go today? I already had an idea. My gut churned, drawing me toward something different. Uncharted territory where I could find a new part of myself, of life. For isn't that a point of it all? "I lose myself and find my soul."

Waves sparkled with a reflection of periwinkle blue and a deep shade dark as night. As the water grew deeper, navigating became a challenge of both mind and spirit, even emotion, working in cohesion, as the waves churned under and around my board in conflicting directions with the shifting winds.

We have to desire the challenge of meeting our very own depths. Riding the course of our inner turmoils to better understand the churning, richly colored dimensions of ourselves, of life. They're a force of nature like these waters themselves.

To meet each wave requires the blending of mind to focus, body to steer course with strength, and spirit to manage the elements coming in and going out. Like the water and the wind that come streaming in without ceasing, like torrents of rain. Or the rhythmic breath that steadies you on your way, your energy expelled into the world around, a force to be reckoned with. It is after all, a deep that's all intimately our own. When we feel ourselves in unison, we can handle the deep. Accomplish the deep. Achieve the deep. Once we do, we will finally be.

Unearthing Dandelions

The sunshine felt good on the bare skin of my shoulders as I flopped the kneeling pad and spade down in the sandy soil of our yard. That quick draining, fine sand, was not too poor in nutrients to scare off the weeds. Those grew in multitude by the year. As I plopped the bag of fresh crocus bulbs I'd purchased onto our lawn, a bright idea put a glint in my eye. For each of these thirty little bulbs I planted, I'd stick them in a spot where a dandelion once was. What a nice way to plant. One less weed, one more flower. That way, if they never come up, at least I still beautified our yard. I shimmied at the genius moment, excited for a good hard job ahead.

The spade was just the tool for the job, but those weeds were aplenty. I didn't have to look hard to choose where to dig. I decided to pick the ugliest monsters to tackle. They were like goliaths.

I had a strategy for attack. Digging my spade straight down into the dirt, I made a circumference around the plant, taking as little ground with each one as possible. I went as deep as the blade would go, trying to get all the taproot. Those big guys tugged out with ease. Every once in a while, I plucked a small one. But then there were a few, some that looked rather normal and I expected to be reasonably simple, that ended up being the hardest to tackle of all! I'd follow my routine only to find that their taproot forked out in different directions and wanted to break off at the end. I had to dig deeper, wider, gentler to master the art of cleanly breaking them free. If not, I'd be leaving a piece behind to start the weed all over again. The beautiful complexity of the human psyche came to mind.

As I encountered this pattern again and again, I began to feel a connection. Digging up these dandelions was a lot like digging into ourselves to extract the weeds that took root in our hearts. Some require simple identification, acknowledgement, and removal. Others, unexpectedly or not, need extra care, gentleness, close attention, more time, to completely remove. Most importantly, a hole cannot be left in their wake. It is necessary to plant new and beautiful things where holes are created in our hearts. That's how we tend to our hearts' gardens.

It's okay to leave some weeds. No garden is perfect. Though weeds are seen as a nuisance that choke out what we want in our soil, environments need plants with taproots, like the dandelion. They serve a purpose to stir things up in soil that has long stood still and stagnant. They unsettle and oxygenate the soil so that new things can grow from deep within sleeping parts of the Earth.

In the soil of my heart, I've uprooted some dandelions and kept others in my soil. Dandelion taproots splayed the different kinds of pains driven in.

The sculpting that those pains did to my character, my thought processes, and my heart are what made me come to understand life as I do. Their complexities taught me how to hold trials and how to hold myself. They oxygenated the soil of my heart because I've learned a deeper compassion, greater balance, truer acceptance, forgiveness, boundaries, discernment, and self-love. Discernment to know which lessons were valuable and what to uproot and plant anew. Like weeds, our gifts in life are seen through how we look at them. Just like the garden of our hearts is tended by how we look into ourselves.

Dandelion Seeds

After a dandelion has been rooted for some time, it goes through its own metamorphosis of sorts. Its flower closes up into a dried spiral having finished taking in the sun in its display. But something is going on beneath the dried surface of its crumpled leaves and petals that appear to be done. Seeds are preparing to unfold in the release of a perfect sphere. As if they'd been there all along waiting to be upheld, because they have been. Waiting for the young child who didn't pick the dandy flower to pull this white and whimsical counterpart and cast their wishes upon the blue sky ahead. With unabashed trust that wish may come with the ability to let that wish go where it may. The innocence to live in the very moment that lies before.

Some dandelions are meant for moments like these. Times when the weeds of scars plant roots of heartache, leaving us feeling crumpled, when hope is dry only to remember that childhood innocence of wishes and trust and faith. When we make a wish in faith, we can let go of its outcome and let the planting of the seed carry it wherever the wind takes that wish, thus taking us. Somehow, that's always far better than where our own begging thoughts lead. It's raw, authentic, purifying, deepening, transformative.

I know that there are many summers to life, just as there are many autumns, winters, and springs. Each one serves its unique purpose. Each one carries with it the promise of wings like these freedoms that carry us.

Some of our gardens' weeds give us the opportunity to share our strength and learning with others who walk a similar road. These transmuting seeds are meant to be cast, to be planted in their hearts in healing and understanding. Touching someone in this way touches us right back. It's a healing that's delivered and received through the deep spiritual gift of heart-learned giving. One that keeps casting another seed gracefully out a little farther into the swirling winds.

Weeding

Children are often some of the people with the purest hearts, untouched yet by the world. They see the beauty in a dandelion. I can't count the times I've been given one as a gift from the schoolyard. Laid upon my desk as a token of love and appreciation.

I think weeds are often a matter of perspective. Some are necessarily a nuisance. Some things need to be weeded for the purpose that they get in the way of living our best life. Only we know which weeds we have and why. Only we know what to do with them to achieve our highest journeys. That's a task done between us and God. So, with the discernment of a gardener, we step foot into our hearts with Him, spade in hand, extract them with tenderness handled with consideration and care, examine our sorrows, feel the contours of their pain where they've grown into our hearts, and treat them with tenderness, for that's the way we truly take their burrowing harm away. When we're through, we feel empowered, for we did it for ourselves, within ourselves, with God by our side, hand in hand. We take in the view of the dandelions left in our earth and know that they are purposeful to our life. We know that some of the most beautiful moments in our lives lie ahead in the opportunities to help someone else see their own dandelion flower, show them how they're growing, what they're conquering, the beauty in their reflection of the sun if only they see their light, their hope, and their dreams. Just like those seeds.

The yellow blossoms radiate sunlight back up to the sky as if to ask, "What defines a flower and a weed?" Are they always so clearly different? Weeds, too, are God's creation. All serve a role. Just as these fine plants have served a role in my life. Both the flowers and the weeds that rooted in my spirit have helped the garden of my heart grow and flourish into who I am now.

Crocus

One fall, I was waiting in line at the general store when I spied flower bulbs marked down in a bin. Sorting through, I found them. Crocuses. There's been a yard that had these peeping from the soil on Elm Street that I passed by nearly every day en route home as a little girl. Their presence put a smile in my heart. They were the first joyful pops of color as spring began to melt the winter snow. I wanted them, stepping back into the line, with a satisfied grin. The customers around me peered into my arms. They reasoned with me that the chances of those flowers rising up out of this earth come spring were questionable if not slim in the extreme northern drifts, where the cold would seep into the space all around them with frost. And that's saying the deer didn't get to them first.

But I couldn't be swayed. I'd already invested in the faith that they would rise even after the weighted drifts of winter's snow. Because that's what they were made to do. They were made to be the first to sprout, sometimes right through those last slushy piles of snow.

God makes us that way too. He makes us to weather the conditions we encounter. And he gives us the power to sprout back up after each cold winter's season with just that same kind of hope and faith in love, in Him. Aren't they one and the same?

After the private winter my heart went through when we moved up north, I felt a wavering faith at times that my heart could bloom. But I'd forgotten. God made me for such a time as this. He made me to not just endure this, but to make beauty out of this. Because I am His. He lives inside me, like the peace and joy and strength and openness in my heart that is an ever part of my spirit. Whenever I go out in nature, I am reminded of this noble truth.

Last fall when I planted each new crocus bulb, I fussed over their winter ahead. I knew mine would be cold too. Little did I know, a few would be lost to the hungry squirrels in a matter of a week, a risk of growing I shrugged, undiscouraged. But after those cold months, a time mostly hunkered inside and alone, and sometimes testing resources, those flowers remembered what they were made for and awakened their power inside. They bloomed.

Bog

As I ventured into the lagoon, the brilliance of nature surrounded me with all its teeming forms of life. A hush fell over what's become a lush green bog of sorts. Only the buzz of dragonflies' wings ushered me into this intimate kingdom no ship could pass. I felt a pointed need to respect the footings of my board, the nature of the water, for this was no longer any human's domain. It was wild, untamed, elusive, and intently unkempt. There was a magic to it that said nature held the reigns here. It gave me pause. At once, I felt privileged to be here yet intrusive of all that it was and for whom.

Some beautiful, dangerous, intimate places are too far to go. It dawned within me. In nature and within the far reaches of a person's self, their spirit, their mind, their memories. There are spaces meant to be left this personal, unkempt, elusive, and exclusive, only to the eyes that see it from within for only they know the dimensions of its landscape, the contours of its story.

I think that's how the navigation of a man goes on a pathway of respect, certainly for this powerful, quiet place. I thought to myself as I deftly turned my board around, heading back to the shores of home, inspired.

The Stars

When I was a little girl, I used to lay awake in bed with amazed, mind-boggled wonder at learning of the infinite number of stars; the unending universe and the idea that there could be more than just us. I wasn't sure if it scared me, impressed me, or just simply sparked my desire all the more to learn and know the world around me. But I've always been drawn to those stars.

Nowhere in the world have I seen with my very own eyes the infinite reaches of those stars and felt them in my bones as I have when I gaze into the pitch-black sky up here. Where the Milky Way's name goes without explaining and in spite of the caring, warning calls of my mother, I find myself drawn to that sky at night unafraid even near the woodsy, wild dark. Sometimes, I'd sneak out of bed just to look out the window and lose track of time gazing out at it. Lose count of the shooting stars that, in reality, don't shoot but rather glide across the void.

Waterways

I crossed the wooden footbridge as I had done so many times before. Memories crossed my mind, some of my own, more fondly of others. As I looked down at the water below, I found myself called to stop, look, and listen to what was taking place beneath me, beneath this wooden bridge. I looked to my left. I looked to my right. Sure there were no cars approaching, I sat down on its edge and peered at the running stream that flowed beneath. Framed in a canopy of trees and branches. Something about the stream captivated me. Made me follow it up its way with attention and appreciation. Listening, wondering thought.

I look down upon the current of the stream and a thought, or even more a feeling, settled into me. Streams flow into brooks. Brooks run into creeks. Creeks into rivers, and rivers into ponds, bays, lakes. Ultimately, every waterway is making its way to the largest body of water it's connected to. Science says the reason is that water is drawn from its source is to replenish the balance in the levels of water around the world.[3] That makes sense. But the feeling is this: We are all humans, by and large, all streams and brooks that gather and flow into these larger bodies of water. Sometimes the appearance of our surface betrays the reality of our tow. We support life in some. We can cause death in others. Sometimes we're transparent, others we're opaque, depending on what's been put into us and around us. When we meet an obstacle, we flow around it or create a gully of depth and dive deeper. Sometimes we rise and sometimes we fall, but we all get where we're going as long as we remember water's key: keep flowing.

---

[3] https://www.usgs.gov/special-topic/water-science-school/science/rivers-streams-and-creeks?qt-science_center_objects=0#qt-science_center_objects

SEASONS OF THE SOUL

Peace of the Night

I wish I could send a bottle of the night air to you. Earth and cedar and pine and life breathes into your lungs in one crisp breath of quiet freshness. Not a sound but the water lapping and the toads croaking softly in the forest. So peaceful. I can barely tear myself away to go to bed.

Viceroys

There are butterflies so like a monarch many can't know the difference. To the untrained eye they look the same. To the trained eye you can see the difference in the way they fly, a daring speed over the lilting flight. A narrow wingtip over the curve of the real thing.

It reminds me that in life and love there are sometimes ruses. We have to be privy to what's around us. Feel not just see. Know and hear. Every sense has something to tell us when we quiet ourselves and pay attention. Once we do that, the truth is plain for all.

Trust in Deep Water

To venture into uncharted waters is an uncomfortable feeling for me. I suppose it is for everyone. But for me, most of all with water. I cannot swim. And because it's not my strong-suit, I do not paddle board into the deep. To do so seems treacherous. Test of fate. A chance of testing my life jacket in a way that invokes fear from a place so primal I can't relate it to another person.

But today, I went. On the cool, smooth water, I pressed my limits. I don't want to live within the walls of my fears, and the only way to tear them down is to push them. So I did. As I paddled, I reached places I could see the dwelling depths, rich with its spiraling weeds that could catch my ankle and drag me in. I passed over areas where plant matter was so rich, I could see only a black with streaks and swirls of emerald green so dark it would swallow you up, never to be found for some time to come. But I didn't allow myself to have those thoughts about those deep reaching places. As I paddled on, I realized trust is a choice. It's knowing the hazards, the risks, and triggers, yet choosing to be brave because it's worth it. You *live* for it. And by that, the rewards far outreach those limiting fears. You push past your own horizons beyond the places you ever imagined and dreamed possible for you. All begins with the deliberate choice of trust. In yourself, in your own lifejacket of sorts, in another, and ultimately in God. All lies in the discerning, deliberate, and empowering choice to trust.

Hawk Song

A red-tailed hawk flew by me, so close I could hear her feathers rustle in her wing beats. She landed in a slumbering tree, her gaze narrowing across the prairie. One would think that prairie too was in a seasonal slumber, but deep beneath the remnants of last year's straw, green grows. A mouse stirs, privy to the danger of the skies. I look out upon this land with a restorative peace. Knowing those who came before me value it as much as I do today. The longevity of this caring shows the common human heart, wild and free, unbridled out in nature this way. What does the soul speak? I listen as I rub the fuzzy new growth of a pussy willow, tenderly. The grass rustles soft timbers you barely hear as a sandhill crane flies overhead, his destination in his heart. The soul leads me here. As quietly as the timbers of this fine prairie grass resounds. A peace settles in my belly as the early evening breeze clears my mind. In my heart is the song of the Redwing blackbird taking flight as it chirps my arrival and takes to song as it flies freely across open skies.

Hush, nature is listening. Exchange the reverence as your spirit speaks with that of the land. I used to fear I'd lost myself in the world so wild and deep in its fervor, so vast and unknown. But it's here I find home. I find home in the solace of the land and the resonance of my own heart beating its way. We are never far from home. All our hearts must do is lean into the wind and let it carry us where it may. I landed here. In these rolling hills of driftless farmland, rich and all their glory of yesteryears and same tomorrows. It's history bleeds through the red of its historic barns, grows in the twisting branches of the old Savannah oaks. Its meanderings show a way not often considered. Aimless wandering. What will you find along the way? For me, I found myself. Unbridled. Restored. Free.

These places awaken my soul.

Finding Fireflies

Blink. Blink. Lights cast neon all around you. Did you see them? One there. Now here. They shine most brightly in the darkest of spaces. Have you ever noticed that? It speaks to me. It tells me that God is like a firefly. As I watch them rise up from the field, they light a glow of magic in my heart. With all the marvel of childhood wonder.

Will you follow the fireflies? Will you chase their flashing glory? Will you stand and look around you at the broader scope? Or simply take in their magic, straight into your spirit as they blink, blink in the night air?

Lightning bugs do not chase. For, just like God's love, the essence of these creatures is to be there. To be joy. Literally illuminating the world with it, just as joy does. And by that, simply being near a lightning bug brings us ancillary feelings of jubilance. Childlike wonder. It's that magic that still exists in our world long after we're children when we take the moment to see it. It's there, a beacon so that we may remember. Just like God.

In the daytime, fireflies are all around. They look like any ordinary beetle roving across any ordinary plant, flying across the pale blue sky. You may not see them, even think of them. But they are there. They're still fireflies, and the role they play in nature is the very same as if we were cognizant of their every move. This is the way we often see God in our good days. The way God works in our lives so intimately and constantly without us needing to ask or even knowing we rely on His role. He is there. Glowing without showing.

In the dark, we feel leery, weary, in need. Fireflies rise up around us, illuminating. It's in this hard time that we see them most clearly, when the sun ne'er lights the day. It's when their presence illuminates our awareness. Much like God's abiding presence. Lightning bugs.

It's when the dark times of our lives traverse our landscapes that we notice. Perhaps we even seek out the little flashes. We chase them, and we want to keep them with us in a jar. Because we feel the magic, the wonder of their presence. We want to be near it, always.

What we forget to remember is that this glow we seek so effortlessly can be felt effortlessly always. God feels your heart. He knows how much you need him at any given moment. He feels what your heart is calling for far beyond what you can articulate. Call upon Him with anything. Know that He's already there; He's been there with you in night and day times, like the light of fireflies. Casting His light to remind you of yours.

You see, when the sun shines on our days, we don't think of fireflies. We don't need their magic, but if they're anything like God, they know we need them. So they fly. They crawl across our boundaries without us even knowing. They seep into our senses only when the day becomes a night. Like a dark night of the soul, that's when God's light teaches us. Shows us that when we reach out to Him, he is there. He has been, but when we reach, as if to catch a firefly and marvel at its shining light, that's when God shows us just how bright that light truly is.

Scientifically speaking, a firefly emits 90% of its energy towards producing light. The human lightbulb uses merely 10% for light.[4] That's not to assert how far man is beneath Him. It's to know that God can handle your burdens. God knows. God will reach you before you have the thought to reach out to Him. He is working, living in you, just like the firefly in the day.

God shines the measure of light needed to illuminate your darkness so that you can feel the glow once more in your heart. Though His work casts glimmers across the dark, we can always feel His presence in the light too, in purposeful flashes of magic, synchronicity, serendipity. Look with faithful eyes. You'll find it. Blink. Blink.

---

[4] https://www.firefly.org/facts-about-fireflies.html

The Glow of Fireflies

Casting shadows in the night only show you your higher truth. Rest in this. You are a firefly too. Everything you do is a reflection of Him. We are all born onto this Earth for a solitary purpose, that is to love. Resting in every heart is the capacity to breathe life into others with their love. That is light. Glow in it. Live love, breathe in it. Know that whenever you feel sorrow, God is there. His firefly's glow casts reminders on your deepest lows that there will be brighter times because you are you, and you are His, cared for, loved. This way for a purpose, glowing your own emission of love that casts magic into every night and quiet goodness into the days. That is you. No matter what form you come in, that's meant to be you. Love you. Be you. But know that by following your glow, truly, you are you. Be your light. Let it glow.

The glow of a firefly casts its joyful light within us. It's as if that light is something that we know we have inside ourselves, and yet we must replenish too in these times. What we must know is that these creatures, like God, are with us no matter whether they are near or far, whether it is day or night in our lives, if only we remember that lightning bugs are not a thing. They are not a place. Nor are they even a person. Are they an idea? I don't think so. Moreso, they are an energy, an omnificent, benevolent, buoyant presence to be known and felt if only we cast our hearts and souls there. God resides within our hearts and souls because He made us. He resides within the day. Within the night. Whenever you look, you'll find that He lives inside you, in the beacon of your own light. And for that, you are a firefly too.

Red-Winged Blackbird

Why does the Redwing blackbird sing? It chirps, it trills, as if speaking to the great unknown. There's a spirit to this land. I can feel it, and I think they can feel it too. Perhaps they speak to it in all their gentle, boisterous ways. Just the same as my heart knows this spirit, centered up on the prairie, the stone wall, the Savannah Oaks, and the Northern Pines. They call to me and I call back to them. Just the same way as the red-winged blackbird sings. Godspeak in the soul.

SEASONS OF THE SOUL

Sunflower

A sunflower. A simple sunflower rising from the earth greets the sun. It says hello, and it lingers there. From the perspective of the sun shining back at it, the flower's face remains there until the dusk calls night to end the day. Whence forth the sunflower waits. For when it's fellow rises again, it will follow. Two faces, mirroring each other in jubilee. Shining in salutation that is steady, ever reaching, always present. For the sun always rises, and the flower always shines its face right back into it. As if, each of their own right, they're sharing a common energy, the mind that illuminates, stores up, and then shares a glory with the world.

When we find our sun, following it comes as naturally and rhythmically as this flower. It's woven into the fiber of our being. It's our inner light that's a part of a greater source, that's shared with everyone, but sometimes especially someone. When we follow our sun, we're greeting a glorious part of our soul. The kind that always lights the day and awaits through the night faithfully.

Epilogue

Every life's journey is a personal process. I hope you've found opportunities to look within yourself and touch the angles of your heart and spirit as you've read these pages. I hope you've gained a greater way of speaking with God and with your soul by nature and the poignant simplicities of life that surround us every day. When we look, listen, and feel, we are inviting ourselves to fully experience our lives and live them aboundingly.

Time goes by far too quickly to simply pass the days. Who makes you feel alive? Spend more time with them. What lightens your heart? Do it often. Where do you feel a sense of home? Go there. In these elements of life, you find your light and the energy to express it. We are all here for a reason. Easy and hard times are inevitable parts of life's process, its seasons. When we make it our intention to be ever-growing through them, garnering lessons along the way, our lives unfold in positive ways, no matter what comes. When we grow, we are bound to blossom. Again and again.

About the Author

As an internationally best-selling author and speaker, Shelby Kottemann founded "Willow Tree: Blossom Heart and Soul" to empower people to experience a greater sense of meaning in daily life. With an emphasis on reflection, relationships, and nature, Shelby leads others to a deepened sense of presence, gratitude, and growth.

To learn more, visit Shelby's YouTube channel. Stay up to date on her upcoming books, coaching, retreats, and distance Reiki healings at shelbykottemann.com.

You may follow Shelby's inspiring posts on Facebook, Instagram, and LinkedIn. You can reach her personally at shelbykottemann@gmail.com.

Books by Shelby Kottemann

Evolution of a Soul

Seasons of the Soul

Books by Shelby Kottemann can be purchased online at Amazon, Apple, Barnes and Noble Online Stores, Books.A.Million, and more.

Reviews

"This excellent author has a creative style of taking her faith in God, her love for nature, and her belief in self worth, and uses this book to demonstrate how the 4 seasons of nature have direct similarities to our lives. With descriptive, powerful art in her words and pictures, she gives structure and empowerment to mind, body and soul. After reading this book, you will have greater knowledge about the beauty of nature and its growth, and be inspired to become the best version of you."

—Toni Stone Bruce, CEO/Founder of Precious Stones 4 Life, LLC, https://www.instagram.com/preciousstones4life/

"I enjoyed the book, *Seasons of the Soul*, by Shelby Kottemann. The book is a collection of thoughtfully arranged vignettes revolving around the seasons of nature. Thought-provoking and whimsical, the author shares a vibrant tapestry of sketches, photographs, musings and observations of the splendor of nature and what it teaches us about ourselves and our lives as we grow and evolve. Lovely work. Thank You."

—Aeriol Ascher, MsD, Positive Vibes with Aeriol Host & Body MindSoul.TV founder www.AeriolAscher.com

"The *Seasons of the Soul* is a breeze that flows through consciousness taking note of nature's beauty and rhythm as it unfolds season to season with various props – trees, cottonwood, spiderwebs and night sky. Each display and word looks at life from a soulful perspective and symbolic reference point. The journey of life – birth, life, decay, death, and release are portrayed in stillness and flow. This book will quiet your soul. It is a comfort that draws you into heart space and revere. Read it when you have blessed yourself with time for reflection."

—Jean Walters, International Best Selling Author https://spiritualtransformation.com/

"As the author Shelby Kottemann writes about life, she poetically does so with the essence of nature and the four seasons. She parallels the journey of life with the changes of Fall, Winter, Spring and Summer. I was touched with her reflection for I am a nature girl and nature is true to my soul. Thank you for bringing to life the Seasons for all of us to read."

—**Karen Wright, International Best Selling Author, Radio Host https://shinenowornever.com/**

"Once again, Shelby has masterfully used nature and faith to teach deep life lessons. This is a marvelous book that should be read, absorbed into your soul, and then lived."

—**Elda Robinson, International Bestselling Author of** *A Simple Cup of -Ty*

www.ingramcontent.com/pod-product-compliance
Lightning Source LLC
Chambersburg PA
CBHW081410080526
44589CB00016B/2522